Numbers Th

By the Numbers:

Because Guesswork is for the Broke

By John Temple

ISBN: 979-8-9927047-6-1
eISBN: 979-8-9927047-7-8

Disclaimer of Liability

This book is provided **as-is**, without any express or implied warranties of financial success, life transformation, or instant millionaire status. While numerology, investing, and financial insights can be powerful tools, results will vary, and no part of this book should be considered financial, legal, or investment advice. The author and publisher assume **no liability** for financial losses, market crashes, business flops, or any regrettable impulse purchases made based on the information contained herein.

Partnership with Ketch Institute of Metaphysics

The author is a proud partner of the **Ketch Institute of Metaphysics**, an organization dedicated to the study and application of numerology, astrology, and other metaphysical sciences in modern life. Through this partnership, the author integrates practical numerology with real-world financial strategies, bridging the gap between ancient wisdom and contemporary investing. The Ketch Institute supports education, research, and practical applications of metaphysical studies, ensuring that numerology is not just an esoteric tool but a valuable method for self-awareness, decision-making, and financial empowerment.

Disclaimer
(Read This Before You Bet Your Life Savings on a Numerology Prediction)

The information in this book is for educational and entertainment purposes only. Yes, numerology can provide fascinating insights into financial patterns, decision-making, and market timing, but no—it **does not come with a crystal ball, lottery-winning secrets, or guaranteed stock market success.** If you're looking for a **get-rich-quick scheme**, you might want to check your Life Path Number for delusion.

Numerology & Financial Guidance

Numerology is a **belief-based system, not a science** (shocking, I know). It can help you identify patterns in behavior, investment habits, and financial timing, but it is not a replacement for logic, financial research, or actual expertise. If you make an investment decision based solely on the fact that it's a "lucky day," well... you might need a **lucky bailout.**

Risk Management (Don't Blame the Numbers)

All investments come with **risk**, whether you're trading stocks, buying real estate, or throwing money at the latest crypto meme coin. This book does **not** guarantee profits, predict stock market crashes, or provide a magic formula for financial success. If it did, I'd be writing this from my private island, not reminding you to **consult a professional** before making major money moves.

- Do your own research.
- Understand that markets are unpredictable.
- Don't put all your money into one investment just because your Personal Year says it's a good time.

Investing & Market Decisions (Use Your Brain, Too)

This book does **not** provide personalized financial, tax, or legal advice. Any strategies mentioned here are ideas to consider, not instructions to follow blindly. Past market trends and numerology patterns are fun to analyze, but they do not guarantee future results. The stock market, economy, and your financial success are influenced by many factors, including luck, timing, and whether or not you panic-sell every time the market dips.

- If you're serious about investing, talk to a certified financial planner.
- If you're thinking about gambling your retirement fund on a "lucky" investment, put this book down and reconsider your life choices.

Business, Real Estate & Legal Considerations

This book touches on business naming, partnerships, and real estate investments from a numerology perspective. But before you:

- Register a company solely based on your Expression Number
- Buy a house because the address "feels lucky,"
- Sign a contract without reading the fine print

...please **consult a lawyer, a financial expert, or at least someone who won't let you make a terrible decision.**

Emotional & Psychological Well-Being

Money can be stressful, and numerology might make you feel better about financial choices, but it is not a substitute for sound financial planning, therapy, or reality. If financial anxiety is keeping you up at night, talk to a licensed professional, not just your horoscope app.

Personal Responsibility (Don't Send Me Angry Emails)

By reading this book, you acknowledge that:

- You are responsible for your own financial decisions.
- The author and publisher are not liable for financial losses, bad investments, or cosmic karma.

- Numerology is a tool, not a fortune-telling service.

Use This Book Wisely

This book is meant to be a guide, a resource, and—let's be real—a fun way to look at money differently. But at the end of the day, your financial future is in your hands. Use common sense, seek expert advice, and don't expect numerology to do all the heavy lifting for you.

Dedication

To **God**, for the wisdom, insight, and ability to bring this book to life. Without divine guidance, this would just be a collection of numbers instead of a roadmap to financial success.

To **Pythagoras**, the O.G. of numerology—thank you for turning numbers into something more than just math class nightmares. Your legacy continues to inspire those of us looking for hidden patterns in the chaos of money and life.

And most importantly, to **you, the reader**—for your curiosity, support, and willingness to explore the power of numbers. May this book help unlock your financial potential and remind you that success isn't just about numbers but about aligning with the right ones.

Here's to wisdom, wealth, and a well-calculated future!

Table of Contents

Preface

Money. That elusive, powerful, and often frustrating thing we all chase. Some people seem to effortlessly attract wealth, while others work themselves into exhaustion just to keep their bank accounts from flatlining. If you've ever wondered why financial success seems to come easier for some people, you're not alone. And no, it's not always because they inherited a trust fund or got lucky with Bitcoin in 2010.

What if I told you that numbers could reveal patterns behind financial success, market cycles, and even your personal ability to build wealth?

Now, before you roll your eyes and assume I'm about to tell you to place your entire retirement fund on a "lucky" lottery number—relax. This is not financial astrology, gambling advice, or some mystical promise that numerology alone will make you rich. This book is about understanding financial patterns, recognizing your strengths and blind spots, and using numerology as a strategic tool for better decision-making.

Numerology: The Hidden Financial Blueprint

For centuries, numerology has been used to predict trends, analyze personalities, and decode the unseen forces at play in our lives. From ancient civilizations to modern investors, numbers have shaped economic cycles, personal fortunes, and global markets. The stock market, real estate booms, business success stories—they all have patterns. And where there are patterns, numerology can provide insight.

This book is designed to take you beyond the basics of numerology and apply it directly to real-world finance and investing. You'll learn how to:

- Discover your Life Path Number and how it influences your financial habits.
- Use numerology to time major financial decisions—investments, business launches, and career moves.
- Identify the best markets for your wealth-building strategy—stocks, crypto, real estate, or passive income.
- Leverage financial cycles and market trends with numerology-based timing.
- Avoid common financial pitfalls based on your personal numerology profile.

But Wait... Is This Book a Guarantee of Wealth?

Absolutely not. If numerology alone could predict the stock market, I'd be writing this from my private island instead of reminding you to use common sense. No system, financial advisor, or market expert can guarantee success. Investing is about strategy, timing, and discipline—not wishful thinking.

However, what numerology *can* do is enhance your financial awareness and help you make better-informed decisions. It can show you why some investments feel natural to you while others lead to frustration. It can help you time financial opportunities based on your unique life cycles. And most importantly, it can give you an edge in understanding wealth-building patterns.

Who This Book Is For

This book is for anyone who wants to build wealth smarter, not harder. Whether you're:

- An investor looking for a unique edge in timing market decisions.
- An entrepreneur wanting to build a financially successful business.
- A real estate buyer seeking the best numerology-aligned properties.
- A trader analyzing price action, Fibonacci retracements, and market cycles.
- Someone just curious about numerology and how it applies to money.

Then you're in the right place. This book blends practical finance, real investing strategies, and numerology principles in a way that is engaging, insightful, and (occasionally) sarcastic. Because, let's face it—money is serious, but learning about it doesn't have to be dull.

So, whether you're a seasoned investor, a skeptical entrepreneur, or just someone looking for a financial advantage, I invite you to dive into the world of numerology-based wealth mastery.

Let's decode your financial future—one number at a time.

Part 1:
Understanding Your Personal Wealth Code

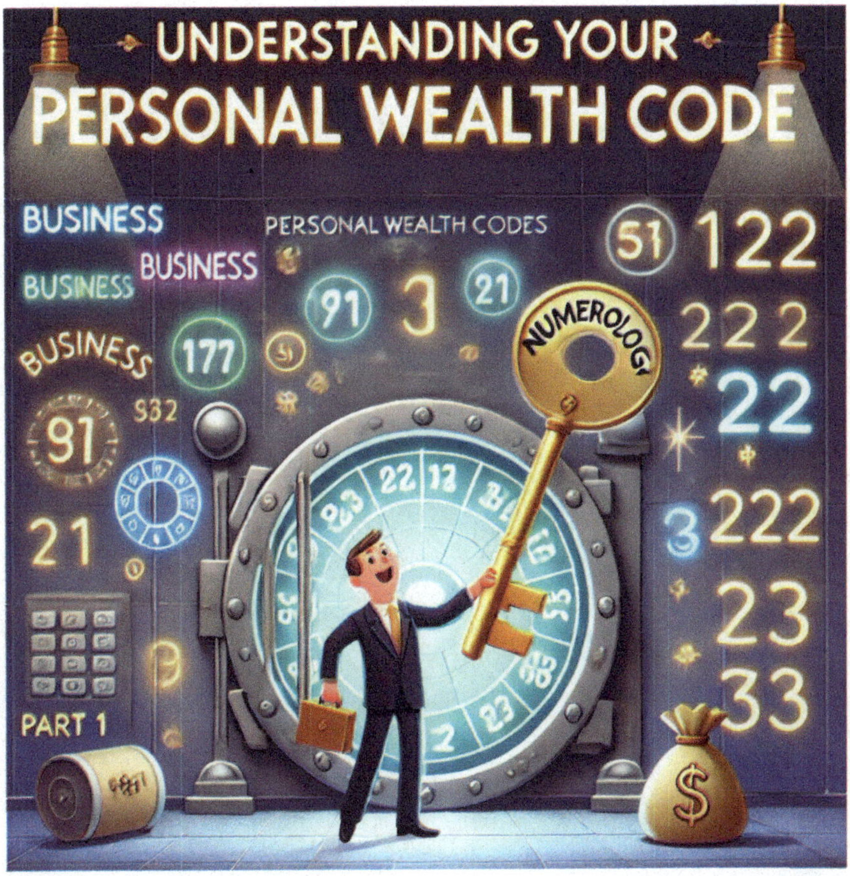

Your Life Path Number & Your Financial Blueprint

Why Your Life Path Number Shapes Your Financial Destiny

Money isn't just about how much you make—it's about how you think, act, and react to financial situations. Some people are natural risk-takers, others are savvy savers, and some somehow manage to lose their wallet at least twice a month.

This isn't random. Your Life Path Number can reveal your natural strengths, financial habits, and even the types of investments that align with your energy.

So, before you make your next big financial move, let's decode your personal wealth blueprint.

How to Calculate Your Life Path Number

This part is easy—no advanced math skills are required. To find your Life Path Number, simply add up the digits of your birthdate until you get a single-digit number (or a Master Number like 11, 22, or 33).

Example: September 15, 1985

Break it down: 9 + 1 + 5 + 1 + 9 + 8 + 5 = 38

Reduce it further: 3 + 8 = 11 (Since 11 is a Master Number, we stop here.)

Life Path = 11

If your final number isn't 11, 22, or 33, keep reducing until you get a single digit (1-9).

Now, let's find out what it means for your financial game plan.

Life Path Numbers & Their Financial Strengths, Weaknesses, and Investment Styles

Life Path 1 – The Independent Leader

Personality & Money Mindset: Natural-born leaders, Life Path 1s are ambitious, self-reliant, and driven by financial independence. They see wealth as a symbol of achievement rather than security.

Ideal Career & Business Paths: Entrepreneurship, executive leadership, tech startups, sales, finance, or anything where they are in control.

Common Financial Mistakes: Impulsiveness in investments, overconfidence leading to risky financial decisions, and difficulty taking financial advice.

Best Types of Investments: Startups, IPOs, high-growth stocks, leadership-based business ventures.

How They Handle Risk & Decision-Making: High risk, high reward—Life Path 1s aren't afraid to take bold financial moves but need discipline to manage their risks.

Wealth Attraction Methods: Create their own business, invest in leadership positions, take calculated risks.

Life Path 2 – The Diplomatic Investor

Personality & Money Mindset: Naturally strategic and patient, Life Path 2s approach finances with caution and careful planning. They prioritize stability over quick wealth.

Ideal Career & Business Paths: Financial advising, legal professions, business partnerships, real estate, human resources, mediation.

Common Financial Mistakes: Fear of taking risks, over-relying on others for financial decisions, and being too conservative.

Best Types of Investments: Dividend stocks, bonds, real estate partnerships, long-term mutual funds.

How They Handle Risk & Decision-Making: Very cautious, prefers low-risk investments but may miss out on big opportunities due to over-analysis.

Wealth Attraction Methods: Build joint ventures, invest with trusted partners, focus on steady and slow wealth-building.

Life Path 3 – The Creative Wealth Builder

Personality & Money Mindset: Highly creative and charismatic, Life Path 3s view money as a tool for expression and lifestyle enhancement.

Ideal Career & Business Paths: Content creation, entertainment, marketing, public speaking, social media influence, design, and artistic ventures.

Common Financial Mistakes: Inconsistent income, lack of budgeting, and overspending on luxuries.

Best Types of Investments: Intellectual property, royalties, online businesses, brand-building.

How They Handle Risk & Decision-Making: Spontaneous risk-takers; may need financial discipline to create long-term wealth.

Wealth Attraction Methods: Monetize creativity, leverage social influence, invest in brands and media platforms.

Life Path 4 – The Disciplined Planner

Personality & Money Mindset: Practical, disciplined, and structured, Life Path 4s approach wealth-building methodically and cautiously.

Ideal Career & Business Paths: Engineering, real estate development, accounting, finance, construction, project management.

Common Financial Mistakes: Overly cautious investing, reluctance to try new financial opportunities, resistance to change.

Best Types of Investments: Real estate, long-term stocks, retirement accounts, index funds.

How They Handle Risk & Decision-Making: Conservative, prefers tried-and-true methods, avoids speculative investments.

Wealth Attraction Methods: Stick to long-term financial plans, invest in tangible assets, and develop multiple income streams.

Life Path 5 – The Freedom-Seeker

Personality & Money Mindset: Life Path 5s are adventurers who thrive on excitement and change. They dislike feeling tied down, which can make financial planning a challenge.

Ideal Career & Business Paths: Travel, sales, consulting, journalism, entertainment, stock trading.

Common Financial Mistakes: Impulsiveness, overspending, and lack of long-term financial planning.

Best Types of Investments: High-growth stocks, cryptocurrency, short-term trading, side hustles.

How They Handle Risk & Decision-Making: Risk-takers by nature but need structure to maintain financial stability.

Wealth Attraction Methods: Diversification, multiple income streams, and adaptable investments.

Life Path 6 – The Responsible Wealth Guardian

Personality & Money Mindset: Life Path 6s are nurturers who prioritize security and stability. They often place family and loved ones before their own financial needs.

Ideal Career & Business Paths: Teaching, healthcare, non-profits, home-based businesses, counseling.

Common Financial Mistakes: Over-giving, reluctance to invest in personal wealth-building.

Best Types of Investments: Real estate, family businesses, long-term retirement plans.

How They Handle Risk & Decision-Making: Cautious and conservative; values stability over aggressive risk-taking.

Wealth Attraction Methods: Focus on sustainable investments and wealth-building for future generations.

Life Path 7 – The Analytical Investor

Personality & Money Mindset: Life Path 7s are deep thinkers who rely on research and intuition. They prefer a methodical approach to wealth-building.

Ideal Career & Business Paths: Science, research, philosophy, technology, investing, financial analysis.

Common Financial Mistakes: Overanalyzing to the point of missing opportunities.

Best Types of Investments: Tech stocks, research-based investments, data-driven trades.

How They Handle Risk & Decision-Making: They prefer calculated risks backed by deep research.

Wealth Attraction Methods: Investing in knowledge-based opportunities and long-term strategies.

Life Path 8 – The Powerhouse Mogul

Personality & Money Mindset: Life Path 8s are natural wealth-builders with a strong drive for success and financial mastery.

Ideal Career & Business Paths: Corporate leadership, finance, real estate, law, business ownership.

Common Financial Mistakes: Becoming overly materialistic or obsessed with control.

Best Types of Investments: Large-scale ventures, real estate, high-value stocks, corporate acquisitions.

How They Handle Risk & Decision-Making: Confident in taking financial risks but must avoid overextension.

Wealth Attraction Methods: Scaling wealth through leadership, ownership, and power investments.

Life Path 9 – The Humanitarian Investor

Personality & Money Mindset: Life Path 9s are visionaries who seek wealth to create positive change in the world.

Ideal Career & Business Paths: Philanthropy, writing, activism, creative industries, social enterprises.

Common Financial Mistakes: Overly generous giving and not prioritizing personal wealth.

Best Types of Investments: Ethical stocks, charitable funds, sustainable business ventures.

How They Handle Risk & Decision-Making: Thoughtful decision-making but can be overly idealistic.

Wealth Attraction Methods: Aligning money with purpose-driven investments and philanthropy.

Master Number 11 – The Intuitive Innovator

Personality & Money Mindset: Master Number 11s are visionary thinkers who attract opportunities through intuition.

Ideal Career & Business Paths: Spiritual guidance, coaching, innovation, artistic fields, leadership.

Common Financial Mistakes: Struggles with grounding financial decisions in practicality.

Best Types of Investments: Impact-driven ventures, creative investments, holistic businesses.

How They Handle Risk & Decision-Making: Intuitive decision-making but needs financial discipline.

Wealth Attraction Methods: Balancing spiritual alignment with practical financial strategies.

Master Number 22 – The Master Builder

Personality & Money Mindset: Master Number 22s are powerful creators who can turn dreams into reality.

Ideal Career & Business Paths: Architecture, engineering, business ownership, large-scale investments.

Common Financial Mistakes: Overcommitting to large projects without financial sustainability.

Best Types of Investments: Real estate, long-term projects, wealth-building enterprises.

How They Handle Risk & Decision-Making: Strategic risk-taking excels in large-scale financial planning.

Wealth Attraction Methods: Leveraging vision and practicality to create lasting wealth.

Master Number 33 – The Visionary Philanthropist

Personality & Money Mindset: Master Number 33s seek financial success as a means to help others and uplift communities.

Ideal Career & Business Paths: Healing professions, education, philanthropy, creative leadership.

Common Financial Mistakes: Difficulty prioritizing personal wealth over collective giving.

Best Types of Investments: Humanitarian efforts, ethical businesses, creative industries.

How They Handle Risk & Decision-Making: Values-driven but may need to focus on personal financial security.

Wealth Attraction Methods: Generating wealth through service-oriented or purpose-driven investments.

How Your Life Path Number Affects Investing & Career Choices

Each Life Path Number approaches money differently. Here's how numerology can help guide your financial journey:

Choosing the Right Investment Strategy → Some numbers thrive in real estate, others in stocks, tech, or entrepreneurship.

Avoiding Financial Pitfalls → Every Life Path has a natural money weakness—learning yours can help you make smarter moves.

Timing Major Financial Decisions → Certain Personal Years are better for taking risks, launching businesses, or saving.

Example: A Life Path 4 & A Life Path 5 Approach Investing

Life Path 4 (Planner) → Prefers long-term, safe investments like real estate or index funds.

Life Path 5 (Adventurer) → Thrives on short-term trades, side hustles, and high-risk opportunities.

Both approaches can work—but knowing your natural strengths lets you align your investment strategy with your personality.

Karmic Debt – The Financial Baggage You Didn't Know You Had

If your financial life feels like a **series of unfortunate events**, you might be carrying **Karmic Debt.** Think of it like an unpaid tab from a past life (or just years of questionable money decisions catching up to you).

Karmic Debt Numbers indicate **lessons you need to learn** before you can **break free from financial struggles and unlock true abundance.** If ignored, they tend to show up as **repeated money problems, financial setbacks, or the inability to hold onto wealth.**

How to Calculate Your Karmic Debt Number

Not everyone has Karmic Debt, but if you do, it'll show up in your **Life Path Number, Expression Number, or Birthday Number.**

Step 1: Check Your Life Path for Karmic Debt

1. Calculate your Life Path Number (sum up your birthdate and reduce to a single digit).
2. If you arrive at **13, 14, 16, or 19 before reducing further**, congratulations—you've got some financial karma to resolve!

Example: If someone was born on **April 25, 1985**:

- 4 + 2 + 5 + 1 + 9 + 8 + 5 = **34** → 3 + 4 = **7** (No Karmic Debt)
- If the result had been **13, 14, 16, or 19 before reducing to a single digit,** that would indicate **Karmic Debt.**

Step 2: Check Your Expression or Birthday Numbers

- If your **full name's numerology calculation** results in **13, 14, 16, or 19**, you might have additional financial karma.
- If you were **born on the 13th, 14th, 16th, or 19th**, that's also a sign you have Karmic Debt to resolve.

What Each Karmic Debt Number Means for Your Finances

13 – The Workaholic Debt

Lesson: Hard work, discipline, and overcoming procrastination.

- **Money Struggles:** Wealth only comes through effort—get-rich-quick schemes will backfire.
- **Fix It:** Stay consistent with money habits, build sustainable income, and avoid financial shortcuts.

14 – The Financial Instability Debt

Lesson: Learning balance, avoiding excess, and managing unpredictability.

- **Money Struggles:** Boom-and-bust cycles, reckless spending, and financial instability.

- **Fix It:** Create a financial plan, embrace moderation, and avoid risky investments.

16 – The Ego-Driven Financial Collapse

Lesson: Overcoming arrogance, material obsession, and learning humility.

- **Money Struggles:** Sudden financial losses due to bad decisions or ignoring red flags.
- **Fix It:** Accept financial responsibility, let go of pride, and seek smart financial advice.

19 – The Self-Reliance Debt

Lesson: Becoming financially independent and taking full responsibility.

- **Money Struggles:** Dependency on others for financial stability, slow progress in wealth-building.
- **Fix It:** Take control of your financial destiny—rely on your own skills, not others.

Breaking Free from Karmic Debt

So, what's the solution? **Face your financial lessons head-on.**

- Recognize patterns in your financial history (are you always struggling in the same way?).
- Commit to making **better, long-term financial decisions.**
- Use numerology to align financial goals with **your strongest numbers.**

Example: Emma had **Karmic Debt 14** and couldn't hold onto money—every time she saved, she **splurged on unnecessary expenses.** Once she **created a structured budget and committed to financial discipline**, she broke the cycle and built real wealth.

Homework: Unlocking Your Wealth Code

Step 1: Calculate your Life Path Number.
Step 2: Identify your strengths & financial challenges.
Step 3: Adjust your investment strategy based on your numerology profile.

Step 4: Use numerology timing to plan major financial moves.
Step 5: Track your progress & refine your wealth-building strategy over time.

Your Financial Blueprint is Unique

Your Life Path Number isn't a financial horoscope—it's a tool. Knowing your strengths and weaknesses can help you navigate financial decisions with confidence.

Up next, we'll dive into how your name influences your money energy—because yes, even your name can affect your financial success.

Are you ready to master your financial destiny? Let's go.

Your Name & Money – The Hidden Power of Numbers in Wealth

Why Your Name Influences Financial Success

Most people assume wealth is just about hard work, smart investments, or a bit of luck. But what if **your name** plays a role in shaping your financial potential? According to numerology, the vibrations of your name influence your **earning potential, financial habits, and business success.**

If you've ever wondered why some people seem to attract wealth effortlessly while others struggle despite doing everything "right," it may come down to their **Expression Number**—the number derived from their full birth name.

Understanding the numerology of your name provides insight into your natural financial tendencies, strengths, and potential challenges. By aligning your name with wealth-attracting vibrations, you can shift your financial trajectory and unlock greater financial success.

How to Calculate Your Expression Number

Your Expression Number (also known as the Destiny Number) is derived from **the full name you were given at birth**. Each letter in your name corresponds to a specific number, which is then totaled and reduced to a **single-digit number (or a Master Number: 11, 22, or 33).**

Numerology Chart for Letters & Numbers:

Letters	A, J, S	B, K, T	C, L, U	D, M, V	E, N, W	F, O, X	G, P, Y	H, Q, Z	I, R
Numbers	1	2	3	4	5	6	7	8	9

Example: Calculating the Expression Number

Let's say your full birth name is **Michael Robert Smith**:

1. Convert each letter to its corresponding number:
    - **Michael** → 4 + 9 + 3 + 8 + 1 + 5 + 3 = **33**
    - **Robert** → 9 + 6 + 2 + 5 + 9 + 2 = **33**
    - **Smith** → 1 + 4 + 9 + 2 + 8 = **24**
2. Add up the total: **33 + 33 + 24 = 90**
3. Reduce to a single digit: **9 + 0 = 9**

Expression Number = **9**

If the final number is 11, 22, or 33, **do not reduce further**, as these are Master Numbers with special significance.

By understanding this number, you can align your financial decisions with your natural strengths and correct potential weaknesses.

Expression Numbers & Their Financial Impact

Expression Number 1 – The Independent Earner

Money Mindset: Highly ambitious, competitive, and driven to be financially independent.

Strengths: Excels in leadership roles, self-employment, and innovation-based industries.

Challenges: Can struggle with teamwork and may take financial risks that backfire.

Best Careers: Entrepreneurs, executives, business owners, tech leaders, sales.

Wealth Strategy: Create personal ventures, take calculated financial risks, and focus on leadership-driven industries.

Ideal Investment Strategies: Venture capital, high-growth stocks, tech startups, and industries where they can take charge.

How They Handle Financial Setbacks: They can be impatient with losses but learn through trial and error. Needs to develop long-term financial patience.

Expression Number 2 – The Cooperative Investor

Money Mindset: Prefers financial security through partnerships and collaborations rather than solo wealth-building.

Strengths: Works well in business partnerships, excellent financial strategist, values financial balance.

Challenges: Can be too reliant on others for financial decisions, sometimes avoids risk to the point of stagnation.

Best Careers: Financial advisors, mediators, counselors, real estate investors, relationship-based industries.

Wealth Strategy: Invest in joint ventures, build strong business relationships, and prioritize long-term financial stability.

Ideal Investment Strategies: Real estate partnerships, dividend stocks, low-risk bonds, and joint business ventures.

How They Handle Financial Setbacks: Prefers a measured approach and may hesitate to cut losses. Benefits from learning to take decisive action.

Expression Number 3 – The Creative Wealth Builder

Money Mindset: Thrives on innovation, values financial freedom, and uses money as a tool for self-expression.

Strengths: Strong communicator, excels in entertainment, branding, and media industries.

Challenges: Can be financially inconsistent due to fluctuating income or lack of structure.

Best Careers: Artists, musicians, designers, influencers, marketers, and public speakers.

Wealth Strategy: Monetize creative talents, diversify income streams, and establish financial discipline.

Ideal Investment Strategies: Intellectual property, online businesses, brand investments, media production.

How They Handle Financial Setbacks: Bounces back quickly by leveraging creativity but must implement structured financial planning.

Expression Number 4 – The Practical Wealth Manager

Money Mindset: Focused on structure, financial discipline, and long-term security.

Strengths: Highly methodical, responsible with money, excellent at financial planning.

Challenges: Can be overly cautious and hesitant to take financial risks.

Best Careers: Engineers, accountants, financial planners, real estate developers, corporate managers.

Wealth Strategy: Build wealth through conservative investments, structured savings, and real estate.

Ideal Investment Strategies: Index funds, real estate, retirement accounts, dividend-paying stocks.

How They Handle Financial Setbacks: They prefer slow recovery strategies and benefit from adapting to market changes.

Expression Number 5 – The Adventurous Investor

Money Mindset: Values financial independence and seeks excitement and high-reward opportunities.

Strengths: Adaptable, excellent at spotting new financial trends and taking advantage of market shifts.

Challenges: Impulsiveness, financial inconsistency, struggles with routine planning.

Best Careers: Travel, sales, consulting, stock trading, marketing, entertainment.

Wealth Strategy: Engage in dynamic investments, embrace flexibility, and seek emerging markets.

Ideal Investment Strategies: High-risk stocks, cryptocurrency, short-term trading, global business ventures.

How They Handle Financial Setbacks: Quick to recover but needs structure to avoid repeating financial mistakes.

Expression Number 6 – The Responsible Wealth Guardian

Money Mindset: Focused on financial security for family and community, prefers stability over risk.

Strengths: Responsible with money, excellent at managing family and group finances.

Challenges: May overextend financial support to others at their own expense.

Best Careers: Healthcare, teaching, counseling, real estate, non-profits.

Wealth Strategy: Secure long-term investments, focus on real estate and legacy wealth-building.

Ideal Investment Strategies: Real estate, insurance, retirement planning, ethical investments.

How They Handle Financial Setbacks: They can be overly cautious but recover well with strategic adjustments.

Expression Number 7 – The Analytical Wealth Strategist

Money Mindset: Prefers well-researched, data-driven financial decisions and relies on deep analysis.

Strengths: Highly intuitive with investments, excellent at spotting long-term trends.

Challenges: Overanalyzes decisions, can hesitate, and miss financial opportunities.

Best Careers: Research, finance, data science, academic roles, financial advising.

Wealth Strategy: Use research-based investing, avoid emotional decisions, and seek undervalued assets.

Ideal Investment Strategies: Technology, biotech, long-term value stocks, precious metals.

How They Handle Financial Setbacks: Overanalyzes losses but eventually finds a rational solution.

Expression Number 8 – The Power Investor

Money Mindset: Naturally attracts wealth, understands financial scaling, and excels at wealth-building.

Strengths: Highly ambitious, great at managing large sums of money and scaling businesses.

Challenges: Can become overly materialistic and may take extreme financial risks.

Best Careers: Business ownership, finance, law, high-level corporate positions.

Wealth Strategy: Scale wealth through bold investments and long-term wealth-building.

Ideal Investment Strategies: Large-scale real estate, hedge funds, high-value stock market investments.

How They Handle Financial Setbacks: Strategically manages losses and rebounds strongly.

Expression Number 9 – The Visionary Philanthropist

Money Mindset: Seeks wealth to benefit humanity and values ethical investments over personal gain.

Strengths: Intuitive with financial decisions, has a strong long-term vision for impact.

Challenges: Can be too idealistic or overly generous with wealth.

Best Careers: Philanthropy, writing, activism, creative industries, social entrepreneurship.

Wealth Strategy: Invest in socially responsible ventures and balance financial sustainability with giving.

Ideal Investment Strategies: Impact investing, sustainable businesses, charitable trusts.

How They Handle Financial Setbacks: Views losses as part of a greater mission but must ensure personal financial stability.

Master Number 11 – The Intuitive Wealth Creator

Money Mindset: Highly intuitive, drawn to visionary financial opportunities, and able to foresee market trends before they become mainstream. They prefer investments that align with their deeper purpose and higher consciousness.

Strengths: Exceptional ability to sense financial shifts, visionary thinking, and strong leadership in innovative fields.

Challenges: Can become overwhelmed by big ideas without proper execution, prone to financial anxiety and over-analysis.

Best Careers: Spiritual coaching, creative direction, leadership roles, consulting, writing, technology startups.

Wealth Strategy: Trust intuition but balance it with logical financial planning. Focus on purpose-driven wealth-building strategies.

Ideal Investment Strategies: Startups, social impact ventures, technology-driven markets, intellectual property.

How They Handle Financial Setbacks: They can be emotionally reactive but recover by realigning financial goals with their deeper purpose. (Expanded details here.)

Master Number 22 – The Master Builder of Wealth

Money Mindset: A natural financial architect capable of creating and managing massive wealth structures. Thinks in terms of long-term financial sustainability and building legacies.

Strengths: Mastery of both financial vision and practical execution, excels in long-term planning, and is highly disciplined.

Challenges: I can become too focused on financial accumulation at the cost of personal well-being and struggle with delegation.

Best Careers: Real estate development, corporate leadership, financial engineering, large-scale business ownership.

Wealth Strategy: Utilize strong organizational skills to develop sustainable investments and business enterprises.

Ideal Investment Strategies: Large real estate holdings, infrastructure projects, private equity, long-term value stocks.

How They Handle Financial Setbacks: Overcomes challenges with persistence and strategic adjustments; capable of rebuilding wealth efficiently. (Expanded details here.)

Master Number 33 – The Philanthropic Visionary

Money Mindset: Views financial success as a means to uplift others and create transformative change in the world. Feels a deep responsibility to use wealth for the betterment of humanity.

Strengths: Compassionate, generous, has strong ethical values in financial decision-making, and excels in humanitarian efforts.

Challenges: Can struggle to balance personal wealth with giving, may prioritize others' needs over financial security.

Best Careers: Non-profit leadership, holistic health, education, public service, philanthropy.

Wealth Strategy: Develop self-sustaining financial systems that allow both personal wealth and large-scale giving.

Ideal Investment Strategies: Ethical stocks, sustainable investments, foundation-based philanthropy, education-focused funding.

How They Handle Financial Setbacks: Views losses as part of a greater learning process but needs to ensure long-term financial sustainability. (Expanded details here.)

Changing Your Name & Financial Energy

Changing your name can lead to a shift in your financial energy, often impacting how opportunities present themselves and how others perceive you in business. Since numerology assigns specific vibrations to names, even small modifications—such as adding a middle initial or shortening your last name—can alter your financial trajectory.

Case Studies of Name Changes and Financial Impact

- **Oprah Winfrey (born Orpah Winfrey):** The slight shift in spelling transformed her brand's memorability, aligning her with success.
- **Jay-Z (born Shawn Carter):** A name change that elevated his business presence beyond music into branding and corporate leadership.
- **Elon Musk (born Elon Reeve Musk):** The streamlined use of his first and last name maintains a powerful numerical energy that aligns with business empires.

Impact of Partial Name Changes

- **Using initials (J.K. Rowling instead of Joanne Rowling)** can create a different public perception, potentially impacting business appeal.
- **Adding or removing a name (e.g., Jennifer Lopez vs. J.Lo)** alters numerological vibrations, influencing financial and personal branding.

Choosing a Name That Enhances Wealth

- Analyze potential name variations and test their numerical outcomes.
- Ensure the new name supports business growth, leadership, and financial energy.

Testing a Name Change Before Committing

- Use different variations on social media and in small business dealings to observe financial shifts.

- Pay attention to intuitive changes in opportunities, financial flow, and professional responses.
- Document changes in financial patterns before and after altering your name.

Legal & Practical Considerations

- Changing your name legally can require significant paperwork and updates to financial accounts.
- Business and brand considerations should ensure numerology aligns with long-term financial strategies.

Choosing a Business Name for Wealth

Choosing the right business name is crucial for financial success. A numerologically aligned name can attract customers, boost profitability, and create long-term stability.

Real-World Examples of Successful Business Names and Numerology

- **Amazon (Expression Number 8):** Aligns with financial power, expansion, and dominance.
- **Apple (Expression Number 5):** Innovation and adaptability in technology.
- **Tesla (Expression Number 6):** Balances visionary leadership with technological advancement.

Matching Name Vibrations to Industry

- **1 (Leadership & Innovation):** Best for startups, personal brands, and trailblazing industries.
- **3 (Creativity & Communication):** Ideal for media, marketing, entertainment, and coaching.
- **5 (Versatility & Global Reach):** Works for travel, tech, and e-commerce companies.
- **8 (Wealth & Authority):** Best for finance, real estate, and high-growth corporations.

Avoiding Bad Name Vibrations

Some numbers bring prosperity, while others create obstacles in business. Here are examples of business names that numerologically may not be beneficial:

- Number 4 (Overly Structured, Slow Growth)
- Number 7 (Spiritual & Isolated, Lacks Commercial Appeal)
- Number 2 (Too Dependent on Others, Lacks Authority)
- Number 9 (Altruistic, But Can Lack Business Focus)

Testing a Business Name Before Launch

- Conduct a numerological analysis of multiple business name variations before filing official paperwork.
- Use surveys and small-scale branding tests to gauge audience engagement and financial potential.

Name Your Wealth

Your name is more than just words—it's a **numerical blueprint that influences your financial potential**. By understanding and harnessing this knowledge, you can align your financial journey with the vibrational energy that supports wealth creation.

With this awareness, you now have the tools to reshape your financial destiny through the power of numerology. The next step is to apply this knowledge, test its effectiveness, and make strategic financial decisions based on your personal name numerology.

From Ancient Markets to Modern Money – The Hidden Influence of Numbers

If you think numerology is just some mystical mumbo-jumbo with no place in finance, **think again**. Ancient civilizations weren't just trading spices and gold—they were using numbers to determine the best time to strike a deal, where to invest, and even how to name their businesses for maximum prosperity.

Long before Wall Street existed, traders, merchants, and rulers relied on **numerical cycles, patterns, and energetic vibrations** to guide financial decisions. Whether you call it superstition or an **early version of economic forecasting**, the fact remains: **numerology has always been tied to wealth-building**.

So, let's take a journey back in time to see how the ancient money masters played the numbers game—and whether we can still apply their methods today.

How Ancient Civilizations Used Numerology in Trade & Investment

Egyptians: When the Pyramids Were Also About Profits

- The **Egyptians** weren't just building pyramids for fun—they were obsessed with **sacred geometry and numerical harmony**.
- Merchants used numerology to determine **auspicious trading days** based on solar and lunar cycles.
- The number **7** (symbolizing divine order) was often used in taxation, trade agreements, and wealth distribution.
- Egyptian traders also developed an **early form of credit**, tied to numerically balanced agreements that ensured fairness in commerce.

Babylonians & Chaldeans: The First Wall Street Analysts?

- The **Babylonians** were notorious for their astrological and numerical forecasting—early investors of their time.
- **Chaldean numerology**, one of the most accurate numerology systems, was developed to predict prosperity and financial success.
- The Babylonians tracked planetary alignments and numbers to determine **the best times to invest in crops, trade routes, and land holdings**.
- They also used **lunar cycles** to regulate market prices and predict economic downturns, much like today's economic cycles.

Chinese Numerology: The Feng Shui of Finance

- In **Chinese numerology**, numbers have deep financial significance.
- The number **8** is considered the luckiest because it represents **infinity, abundance, and unbreakable financial flow**.
- Businesses in China often pay huge sums to have the number **8** in phone numbers, addresses, and stock listings.
- The number **4**, however, is avoided in financial matters as it sounds like the word for "death"—which is never a great vibe for money.
- The Chinese developed **auspicious date selection** for launching businesses, signing contracts, and investing based on numerical cycles.

The Greeks & Pythagoras: The OG Data Analysts

- The famous mathematician **Pythagoras** (yes, the guy who tormented you in geometry class) didn't just mess with triangles—he created **Pythagorean numerology**.
- The Greeks believed numbers had intrinsic **vibrational properties** that influenced wealth, health, and success.
- **Pythagorean numerology** became the foundation for modern numerology systems, linking numbers to personality traits and financial potential.
- Greek philosophers used numerology to **advise rulers and business leaders on optimal financial decisions**.

Hindu Numerology & Vedic Astrology: Cosmic Investing

- Ancient **Indian traders and kings** consulted numerology and **Vedic astrology** before making major economic moves.
- The number **9**, associated with **Mars**, was considered powerful for initiating ventures that required aggression, competition, and rapid financial growth.
- **Lunar and planetary cycles** were heavily used to determine **auspicious investment windows**.
- The **Nakshatra system** in Vedic astrology guided investment timing based on planetary movements.
-

Mayan & Aztec Numerical Systems: The Calendar of Cash Flow

- The **Mayans** had one of the most advanced mathematical systems, using **base-20 numerology**.
- They tracked cycles of abundance and scarcity through their elaborate calendar, using it to predict **economic booms and downturns**.
- Similar to today's economic cycles, the Mayans knew when to store resources and when to **take financial risks**.
- The **Tzolk'in calendar** helped traders decide the best periods for commerce and expansion.

Pythagorean vs. Chaldean Numerology – Which One Predicts Wealth Best?

Pythagorean Numerology: The Numbers You Know

- Developed by **Pythagoras**, this system assigns numbers **1-9** to letters in a straightforward way (A=1, B=2, C=3, etc.).
- It is widely used in personal numerology, business names, and modern financial applications.
- Great for **personal wealth analysis** and understanding long-term financial habits.
- Used in modern stock market cycles and trading strategies based on numerical forecasting.

Chaldean Numerology: The Mysterious & Ancient System

- Uses a different number assignment, based on **vibrational frequencies**, with numbers 1-8 (no 9, as it is considered sacred).
- Considered **more accurate for predicting financial events** but more complex.
- Used by ancient merchants to **determine lucky business names, financial cycles, and investment timing**.
- Some modern businesses still use **Chaldean numerology** to optimize brand names and financial growth.

Which One Should You Use?

- **Pythagorean** numerology is great for understanding your **personal financial habits**.
- **Chaldean** numerology is better for **business success, naming, and forecasting cycles**.
- Want the best of both worlds? **Use both systems** for deeper insights (think of it as financial due diligence, but numerology-style).

Are Other Metaphysical Tools Relevant to Finance?

Astrology & Finance – The Stock Market's Worst-Kept Secret

- Many traders and financial experts use **planetary cycles to predict market movements**.
- Jupiter cycles align with **economic expansion**, while Saturn cycles often signal **economic slowdowns**.
- Some of the biggest market crashes have aligned with **Mercury retrograde periods** (coincidence or conspiracy?).
- **Financial astrologers** analyze planetary transits to predict stock market booms and busts.

Tarot & Intuition-Based Investing

- Believe it or not, some successful investors use **tarot cards** to confirm financial decisions.
- The **Wheel of Fortune** card? Probably a good day for trading.
- The **Tower** card? Maybe don't check your crypto portfolio.
- Some hedge fund managers use **intuitive investing techniques** that combine traditional finance with metaphysical insights.

Can Numbers Really Predict Wealth?

While modern economists might scoff at numerology, **history says otherwise**.

From **ancient kings to Wall Street investors**, numbers have always played a role in finance. Whether it's predicting stock market cycles, choosing business names, or just **not launching a startup in a Personal Year 9**, numerology can be a **powerful financial tool**.

So, the next time someone calls numerology nonsense, remind them that **billionaires still check lucky numbers before sealing major deals**—and maybe, just maybe, they know something the rest of us don't.

Wealth Mindset & Numerology – Rewiring for Success

Why Some People Naturally Attract Money While Others Struggle

Ever met someone who seems to **effortlessly attract wealth**—as if they were born with a money magnet embedded in their soul? Meanwhile, others can hustle day and night, only to find themselves stuck in a never-ending financial hamster wheel? Is it just **luck, fate, or an unfair cosmic joke?** Nope—it's all about **money mindset and numerical energy**.

Your **core numerology numbers** influence your financial patterns more than you think. Just like some people are naturally gifted in music or athletics, others are numerically wired to excel in financial matters. But here's the good news: **You can rewire your money mindset using numerology** to break free from financial struggles and attract abundance.

The Numerology of Wealth Attraction

Each number carries a unique energetic vibration that affects your **relationship with money**. Some numbers are **naturally aligned with wealth-building**, while others must do some inner work to break through financial blocks. Understanding these influences can help you **identify and shift** limiting money beliefs.

Life Path & Wealth Energy

Your **Life Path Number** (calculated from your birthdate) plays a significant role in how you approach financial success. Let's break down what each number says about **your financial tendencies**:

- **Life Path 1:** Independent and entrepreneurial but may struggle with teamwork and delegation in financial matters.
- **Life Path 2:** Naturally collaborative but can be overly reliant on financial partnerships rather than building personal wealth.
- **Life Path 3:** Creative and expressive, thrives in industries that involve communication and art but must learn financial discipline.
- **Life Path 4:** The planner—great at saving and long-term investments but needs to take more calculated financial risks.
- **Life Path 5:** The adventurer—attracts money easily but must learn to manage it wisely and avoid impulsive financial decisions.
- **Life Path 6:** Generous and responsible, but may prioritize others' financial needs over personal wealth-building.
- **Life Path 7:** Analytical and intuitive—great at research-based investing but needs to avoid overthinking financial decisions.
- **Life Path 8:** The power player—naturally attracts money and wealth opportunities but must balance ambition with responsibility.
- **Life Path 9:** The giver—wants to use wealth for a higher purpose but must ensure personal financial stability first.
- **Master Number 11:** The intuitive wealth creator—financial success comes from bold, visionary ideas but needs to balance big dreams with real-world execution.
- **Master Number 22:** The master builder—can create long-lasting financial empires but must avoid overworking and burnout.

- **Master Number 33:** The wealth philanthropist—money flows easily when it's tied to service, but you must remember that charity begins with financial security.

How to Break Limiting Money Beliefs Using Numerology

Many people struggle financially not because they lack opportunities but because they subconsciously block their own success. These blocks often stem from past conditioning, societal beliefs, or even inherited money patterns from family. Numerology provides a powerful tool for identifying and overcoming these blocks.

Step 1: Identify Your Money Blocks by Number

Each person has a unique set of **financial challenges** based on their numerology. Here's how different numbers might struggle with money and what they can do to break free:

- **If your core number is 1:** You may believe you have to do everything alone. Example: *Emma refused to hire a financial planner, thinking no one could handle her money as well as she could. Once she sought expert advice, her wealth grew exponentially.*
- **If your core number is 2:** You might feel uncomfortable making independent financial decisions. *Example: Daniel constantly second-guessed his investments, relying on others' opinions. When he started trusting his research, he made profitable choices.*
- **If your core number is 3:** You love spending and may avoid structured financial planning. *Example: Olivia always spent her earnings on spontaneous trips and luxury items. When she started budgeting, she was able to enjoy life while saving.*
- **If your core number is 4:** You may fear financial instability and avoid taking necessary risks. *Example: Mark kept his money in low-interest savings accounts, afraid of investments. Once he took a calculated risk, he saw significant growth.*
- **If your core number is 5:** You embrace financial freedom but may lack consistency. *Example: Sophia jumped from one money-making scheme to another without sticking to a plan. After setting clear financial goals, she achieved long-term stability.*

- **If your core number is 6:** You put others' financial needs before your own. *Example: Sarah drained her savings by helping family members instead of securing her future. Once she set financial boundaries, she built personal wealth while still helping others.*
- **If your core number is 7:** You overanalyze money decisions and delay action. *Example: John spent years researching investments but never pulled the trigger. When he finally acted on a solid strategy, he started seeing real financial progress.*
- **If your core number is 8:** You may focus too much on material success, neglecting emotional fulfillment. *Example: James chased status symbols but felt empty inside. When he redirected his wealth toward meaningful experiences, he found true prosperity.*
- **If your core number is 9:** You tend to give away money too freely. *Example: Lisa donated excessively, leaving herself in financial trouble. When she balanced giving with smart investing, she secured her future while still supporting the causes she loved.*
- **Master Number 11:** You get financially paralyzed by too many ideas. *Example: David had endless investment ideas but never followed through. Once he committed to one strategy, his business soared.*
- **Master Number 22:** You want to build *everything*—business, charity, legacy. *Example: Michelle tried launching multiple businesses at once and burned out. When she focused on one scalable venture, she succeeded.*
- **Master Number 33:** You try to save the world before securing your own financial future. *Example: Alex funded charitable projects at the expense of his own stability. When he built sustainable income streams first, he could give even more.*

Step 2: Use Numerology to Shift Your Wealth Mindset

Now that you've identified your **money blocks**, it's time to **reprogram your financial mindset** using numerology. Here's how:

1. Affirmations Based on Your Numbers

Each Life Path Number has specific **affirmations** that help rewire financial beliefs.

- ***Life Path 1:*** "I confidently create financial independence." *Example: Emma, a Life Path 1, struggled with trusting employees in her startup. When she finally delegated, her business grew exponentially.*
- ***Life Path 2***: "I trust myself to make smart financial decisions." *Example: Daniel, a Life Path 2, always second-guessed his investment choices. When he started following a structured plan, his wealth doubled.*
- ***Life Path 3:*** "I balance creativity with financial responsibility." *Example: Olivia, a Life Path 3, loved spending on passion projects. Once she set a strict budget, she found a way to fund creativity and grow her savings.*
- ***Life Path 4***: "I take strategic risks that grow my wealth." *Example: Mark, a Life Path 4, was overly cautious. When he started taking small investment risks, he realized higher financial returns.*
- ***Life Path 5:*** "I embrace financial stability while enjoying my freedom." *Example: Sophia, a Life Path 5, loved jumping into new investments but lacked discipline. She automated her finances and kept her adventurous spirit.*
- ***Life Path 6:*** "I prioritize my financial success along with helping others." *Example: Sarah, a Life Path 6, always put family needs above her own. Once she prioritized her wealth, she was able to help others more sustainably.*
- ***Life Path 7:*** "I trust my intuition and take decisive action in finances." *Example: John, a Life Path 7, hesitated on stock market investments. When he trusted his research and intuition, he started making better financial decisions.*
- ***Life Path 8:*** "I attract wealth with confidence and purpose." *Example: James, a Life Path 8, was driven by material success but felt unfulfilled. When he aligned wealth with his values, he found true prosperity.*
- ***Life Path 9:*** "I manage my wealth wisely while contributing to the greater good." *Example: Lisa, a Life Path 9, gave away money too freely. When she balanced giving with saving, she created a lasting impact.*
- ***Master Number 11:*** "I turn my visionary ideas into profitable realities." *Example: David, a Master Number 11, had big ideas but no execution. When he focused on one project, his success skyrocketed.*
- ***Master Number 22:*** "I build lasting wealth with focus and patience." *Example: Michelle, a Master Number 22, wanted to build an empire overnight. When she embraced a long-term strategy, her business flourished.*
- ***Master Number 33:*** "I create financial abundance to serve both myself and the world." *Example: Alex, a Master Number 33, kept giving without securing*

his finances. Once he created a sustainable wealth plan, he could give even more.

---

2. Align Your Personal Year Number with Wealth Strategies

Each year, you move through a **Personal Year Cycle** that influences your financial success. Align your money strategies accordingly.

- ***Personal Year 1:*** Great for starting new financial ventures. *Example: Sarah used her Personal Year 1 to launch her dream business, which became her most profitable venture ever.*
- ***Personal Year 2*:** Best for financial partnerships and planning. *Example: Jacob strengthened his business partnerships and negotiated lucrative deals in his Personal Year 2.*
- ***Personal Year 3*:** A creative money-making year, but avoid reckless spending. *Example: Emily monetized her creative skills in Personal Year 3 but had to resist overspending on luxuries.*
- ***Personal Year 4:*** Focus on saving, budgeting, and long-term investments. *Example: Thomas doubled his retirement contributions and started a disciplined savings plan.*
- ***Personal Year 5:*** A year of financial surprises—stay adaptable. *Example: Ava capitalized on unexpected opportunities, shifting her investments to high-growth stocks.*
- ***Personal Year 6*:** Invest in home, family, and security. *Example: Ryan bought a home and set up financial safety nets for his family.*
- ***Personal Year 7:*** Research finances but avoid hasty decisions. *Example: Nathan spent his Personal Year 7 studying wealth-building strategies instead of rushing investments.*
- ***Personal Year 8:*** Peak wealth-building—take bold actions. *Example: Olivia expanded her business and doubled her net worth in Personal Year 8.*
- ***Personal Year 9*:** Wrap up financial projects and let go of bad investments. *Example: David sold underperforming assets and cleared debts to prepare for his next cycle.*
- ***Master Number 11 Year*:** A time for inspired financial breakthroughs—trust your intuition but ground it in strategy. *Example: Maria's intuitive stock picks paid off after she combined research with her gut feelings.*

- ***Master Number 22 Year***: The ultimate wealth-building year—major investments, long-term growth, and financial empire expansion. *Example: Michael expanded his business into international markets during his Personal Year 22.*
- ***Master Number 33 Year:*** A year to balance financial success with giving back—money flows when purpose aligns with wealth. *Example: Anna launched a profitable nonprofit venture in her Personal Year 33, aligning wealth with service.*

Mastering Money with Numerology

Attracting wealth isn't just about working hard—it's about **aligning your mindset, actions, and energy with abundance**. By understanding how your numerology influences financial habits, you can reprogram your subconscious, eliminate self-sabotaging beliefs, and unlock **your full wealth potential**.

The next step? **Apply these insights in real life**—adjust your financial strategies, use affirmations, and start confidently moving towards financial abundance. Your numerology numbers are not just numbers; they're your blueprint for success.

Everyday Numerology – Making Smarter Money Moves

Timing is Everything (And Yes, The Universe Knows It Too)

If you've ever wondered why some days you feel like a financial genius and others you can barely figure out your Venmo balance, it's not just bad luck—it's numerology. Whether it's signing a contract, launching a business, or making an investment, **picking the right day can make or break your financial success**.

That's where **Personal Day, Month, and Year Numbers** come in. Instead of blindly throwing money at the market or making a career move on a whim, you can align your financial decisions with **numerology-backed timing**—why not stack the odds in your favor?

Personal Year, Month & Day Numbers: Your Financial Weather Forecast

Numerology isn't just about long-term cycles; it's also about **daily and monthly timing**. Just like the stock market has bull and bear trends, **your personal numbers shift** to influence how smoothly (or chaotically) things go. Think of it as your own **financial weather forecast**—you wouldn't plan a beach trip in the middle of a storm, so why make major financial moves on an off-day?

How to Calculate Your Personal Year Number

This is your **big-picture theme for the year**, influencing everything from career growth to financial breakthroughs.

1. Add your birth month and birth day together.
2. Add the current year's digits together.
3. Add the two totals and reduce to a single digit (or Master Number 11, 22, 33).

Example:

If you were born on **April 5** and you want to calculate your **Personal Year for 2025**:

- Birthdate: **4 + 5 = 9**
- Current Year: **2 + 0 + 2 + 5 = 9**
- Total: **9 + 9 = 18 → 1 + 8 = 9**

Your **Personal Year Number** for 2025 would be **9**—a year for **wrapping up projects, selling off assets, and preparing for a fresh start**.

How to Calculate Your Personal Month Number

Your **Personal Month Number** fine-tunes your financial timing, showing you which months are best for taking action versus sitting tight.

1. Take your **Personal Year Number** and add it to the current month.
2. Reduce to a single digit (or Master Number 11, 22, 33).

Example:

If your **Personal Year Number** is **9** and you're checking for **July (7th month):**

- 9 + 7 = 16 → 1 + 6 = 7
- July is a 7 Month for you—great for learning, analyzing finances, and planning, but not ideal for major investments.

How to Calculate Your Personal Day Number

Your **Personal Day Number** tells you if today is the day to **make money moves or hide under a financial blanket**.

1. Take your **Personal Month Number** and add it to the current day.
2. Reduce to a single digit (or Master Number 11, 22, 33).

Example:

If your **Personal Month Number** is **7** and today's date is the **14th**:

- 7 + 14 = 21 → 2 + 1 = 3
- Today is a 3 Day for you—perfect for networking, creative money-making, and marketing. Not the best for signing serious contracts.

What Each Number Means for Your Money Moves

Now that you know how to calculate your **Personal Year, Month, and Day Numbers**, here's what they mean for your financial decisions:

- **1** – Best for **starting fresh**: New job, new investment, business launch.
- **2** – Best for **planning & partnerships**: Signing contracts, making financial collaborations.
- **3** – Best for **creativity & expansion**: Marketing, brand building, side hustles.
- **4** – Best for **stability & structure**: Saving money, building assets, long-term investments.
- **5** – Best for **opportunities & risks**: Trying new investments, business expansions.
- **6** – Best for **home & family wealth**: Real estate purchases, financial planning.
- **7** – Best for **reflection & research**: Studying market trends, making future plans.

- **8** – Best for **money-making & power moves**: Promotions, high-stakes investments.
- **9** – Best for **ending cycles & cashing out**: Selling property, paying off debts.
- **Master Number 11** – Best for **inspired financial decisions**: Big breakthroughs, intuitive investments.
- **Master Number 22** – Best for **building empires**: Major business growth and financial scaling.
- **Master Number 33** – Best for **giving back & purpose-driven wealth**: Philanthropy, impact investing.

Choosing Dates for Contracts, Investments, and Career Moves

If you've ever signed a contract on a bad day and regretted it later, **numerology could've saved you the headache**. Picking the right date for financial milestones isn't just a superstition—it aligns your energy with the best possible outcomes.

Best Days for Business & Investing

- ***Personal Day 1 or 8*** – Ideal for signing contracts, launching businesses, making investments. *Example:* Emma, a Life Path 1, signed her business incorporation papers on a Personal Day 1, aligning with her leadership energy, and her startup took off quickly.
- ***Personal Day 4 or 6*** – Best for stability-focused money moves (buying property, setting up savings plans). *Example:* James, a Life Path 4, closed on his first rental property on a Personal Day 4. The deal was solid, and the property appreciated significantly over time.
- ***Personal Day 5*** – Great for seizing **fast-moving financial opportunities**, but risky for long-term commitments. *Example:* Olivia, a Life Path 5, took a calculated risk by investing in cryptocurrency on a Personal Day 5. She saw big gains—but also learned to cash out at the right time.
- ***Personal Day 7*** – **NO big financial moves** today. Research, reflect, and plan instead. *Example:* Nathan, a Life Path 7, avoided signing an investment deal on a Personal Day 7, choosing instead to review the fine print. He later found a flaw that saved him thousands.

Best Days for Job Changes & Career Growth

- ***Personal Day 1*** – Apply for jobs, ask for a raise, step into leadership. *Example:* Maria, a Master Number 11, scheduled her job interview for a Personal Day 1. She got the position and a salary increase aligned with her vision.
- ***Personal Day 3*** – Public speaking, creative pitches, networking events. *Example:* David, a Life Path 3, gave a TED Talk on a Personal Day 3. His brand skyrocketed, bringing in new clients.
- ***Personal Day 8*** – High-powered career moves, salary negotiations. *Example:* Robert, a Life Path 8, negotiated a major promotion on a Personal Day 8, securing a leadership role and a six-figure salary.

Worst Days for Major Financial Decisions

- ***Personal Day 9*** – Not a time to start new things. Closeout projects instead. *Example:* Lisa, a Life Path 9, learned the hard way by investing in a startup on a Personal Day 9. The business soon folded, confirming that 9 is a number of endings, not beginnings.
- ***Personal Day 7*** – Deep thinking, not deep investing. *Example:* Mark, a Master Number 22, planned to buy stocks but felt hesitant on a Personal Day 7. He later realized the market crashed that same day, dodging a financial loss.
- ***Personal Day 2*** – Negotiations are fine, but **don't rush into decisions**. *Example:* Sophie, a Life Path 2, tried to push forward a business merger on a Personal Day 2. The contract later revealed hidden fees she hadn't noticed in her rush.

Master Numbers & Their Ideal Money Moves

- ***Master Number 11 Day*** – Best for intuitive business moves, creative investments. *Example:* Jake, a Master Number 11, invested in an AI startup on a Personal Day 11, following his gut. The company later became a major industry leader.
- ***Master Number 22 Day*** – Perfect for long-term financial planning, wealth-building strategies. *Example:* Michelle, a Master Number 22, launched her financial coaching business on a Personal Day 22, setting herself up for legacy wealth.

- ***Master Number 33 Day*** – Great for philanthropy, impact investing, and wealth redistribution. *Example:* Alex, a Master Number 33, donated to an organization on a Personal Day 33, and later found himself attracting unexpected financial rewards.

If you've ever signed a contract on a bad day and regretted it later, **numerology could've saved you the headache**. Picking the right date for financial milestones isn't just a superstition—it aligns your energy with the best possible outcomes.

Best Days for Business & Investing

- ***Personal Day 1 or 8*** – Ideal for signing contracts, launching businesses, making investments.
- ***Personal Day 4 or 6*** – Best for stability-focused money moves (buying property, setting up savings plans).
- ***Personal Day 5*** – Great for seizing **fast-moving financial opportunities**, but risky for long-term commitments.
- ***Personal Day 7*** – **NO big financial moves** today. Research, reflect, and plan instead.

Best Days for Job Changes & Career Growth

- ***Personal Day 1*** – Apply for jobs, ask for a raise, step into leadership.
- ***Personal Day 3*** – Public speaking, creative pitches, networking events.
- ***Personal Day 8*** – High-powered career moves, salary negotiations.

Worst Days for Major Financial Decisions

- ***Personal Day 9*** – Not a time to start new things. Closeout projects instead.
- ***Personal Day 7*** – Deep thinking, not deep investing.
- ***Personal Day 2*** – Negotiations are fine, but **don't rush into decisions**.

Planning Recurring Financial Events with Numerology

Just like you wouldn't schedule a dentist appointment during a Mercury retrograde (unless you enjoy communication mishaps and painful drills), timing

recurring financial events with numerology can smooth out cash flow and keep you from unexpected hiccups.

- **Best Personal Days for Setting Up Auto-Pay & Savings Plans:**
  - **4 or 8** – Financial stability and structured planning.
  - **6** – Ideal for home-related savings and long-term security.
  - **Master Number 22** – Best for setting up **legacy-building financial systems**.

Example: Mark, a Life Path 8, switched his bill payments to process on Personal Day 8 every month. Somehow, late fees mysteriously disappeared, and his financial stress levels hit an all-time low.

Credit Score & Numerology – The Hidden Connection

Ever wondered why some people seem to breeze through loan approvals while others get rejected faster than a bad Tinder date? Numerology might have something to say about that.

- **Numbers in your credit score can influence your financial stability.**
  - If your credit score reduces to a **4 or 8**, you likely have a stable foundation.
  - A **5 or 9** could indicate unpredictable financial swings.
- **Best Personal Days to Pay Off Debt or Apply for Loans:**
  - **1 or 8** – Initiating financial independence or securing power moves.
  - **Master Number 11** – If your intuition screams "YES" on this day, trust it.

Example: Olivia, a Life Path 5, struggled with her fluctuating credit score. She started making debt payments on Personal Days 4 and 8, and suddenly, her financial situation started stabilizing like a well-balanced stock portfolio.

Shopping & Large Purchases – Numerology for Smart Spending

Retail therapy is fun—until your bank account files for emotional distress. Use numerology to **time big-ticket purchases wisely** and avoid impulse-buying regret.

- **Best Personal Days to Buy Expensive Items:**
  - **3** – Great for splurging on something fun (but don't go overboard).

  - **6** – Ideal for purchasing home-related goods and real estate.
  - **8** – Power shopping: buy investment pieces that hold long-term value.

Example: James, a Life Path 3, nearly impulse-bought a ridiculously expensive watch on a Personal Day 5 (chaotic energy). Instead, he waited for a Personal Day 8 and got it **on sale**—talk about winning the numbers game!

Travel & Financial Timing – Making Money Moves on the Go

If you're planning a trip for business, networking, or scouting new investment opportunities, **numerology can help you choose the best time** to pack your bags.

- **Best Personal Days for Travel & Business Networking:**
- **5** – Great for movement, adventure, and fresh opportunities.
- **7** – Best for spiritual retreats, learning experiences, and self-reflection.
- **Master Number 22** – Excellent for **business travel with serious financial potential**.

Example: Sophia, a Life Path 5, scheduled her international investment trip on a Personal Day 5. She ended up meeting a business partner by "coincidence" and landed a lucrative real estate deal. Coincidence? Not according to numerology.

Emergency Funds & Unexpected Expenses – What Your Numbers Say

Life happens. Cars break down, surprise medical bills show up, and that *totally-worth-it* vacation suddenly costs double. **Numerology can help you prepare for financial surprises before they happen.**

- **Best Personal Years & Months for Building an Emergency Fund:**
  - **4 or 6** – Stability-focused years, ideal for financial protection.
  - **8** – Wealth accumulation and fortifying assets.
  - **Master Number 11** – If you sense **a financial storm brewing**, prepare in advance.

Example: Rachel, a Life Path 6, started her emergency fund on a Personal Day 4. A few months later, she had a medical expense pop up—but guess what? **She was fully prepared.**

Final Thoughts: Timing Your Way to Wealth

The biggest lesson here? **Not all days are created equal when it comes to money.** By aligning your financial decisions with your **Personal Year, Month, and Day Numbers**, you can make **smarter, better-timed money moves** instead of playing financial roulette.

So, before you go making bold investments or quitting your job for a "fresh start," check your numbers. Because let's be real—when it comes to wealth, **timing is everything**.

Business Success & Numerology – Branding, Growth & Partnerships

Why Some Businesses Thrive (And Others Flop Faster Than a Bad IPO)

If you think business success is all about having a revolutionary idea, let me introduce you to the **thousands of failed startups** that had "game-changing" concepts and still ended up in the financial graveyard. The truth is, **timing, branding, and partnerships matter**—and guess what? Numerology plays a huge role in all of them.

Whether you're starting a new company, looking for a co-founder, or wondering why your business is stuck in the financial mud, **numerology can help you get your numbers in order—literally**.

How Numerology Helps Pick the Right Business Partners

Business partnerships can be the best decision of your life—or the worst. (Think Apple's Steve Jobs and Steve Wozniak vs. the disastrous AOL-Time Warner merger.) Just like personal relationships, **some numbers work well together, while others create financial and legal nightmares**.

Step 1: Calculate Your Business Partner's Core Number

You don't want to **merge your financial fate** with just anyone, right? Before signing contracts, take a moment to check the numerological **compatibility** of your potential partner. Here's how:

1. Take their full birthdate.
2. Add up all the digits.
3. Reduce to a single digit (or Master Number 11, 22, 33).

Example: If Sarah was born on March 5, 1986:

- **3 + 5 + 1 + 9 + 8 + 6 = 32 → 3 + 2 = 5**
- Sarah's core number is **5.**

Now, let's check how **her number aligns with different business styles.**

Best & Worst Business Partner Matches by Number

- **1** – Best with **3, 5, 8** (Strong leadership but avoid clashing with other 1s.)
- **2** – Best with **4, 6, 8** (Great for partnerships but may struggle with indecisiveness.)
- **3** – Best with **1, 5, 7** (Creative but needs structured numbers for balance.)
- **4** – Best with **2, 6, 8** (Great for stability but slow to take risks.)
- **5** – Best with **1, 3, 7** (Thrives on flexibility but struggles with structure.)
- **6** – Best with **2, 4, 8** (Excellent for long-term business growth.)
- **7** – Best with **3, 5, 9** (Ideal for research-based or intuitive businesses.)
- **8** – Best with **1, 2, 4** (Money-driven but needs ethical balance.)
- **9** – Best with **6, 7, 11** (Purpose-driven, great for philanthropy.)
- **Master Number 11** – Best with **7, 9, 22** (Ideal for visionary businesses.)
- **Master Number 22** – Best with **4, 8, 33** (Builds empires, needs practical execution.)

- **Master Number 33** – Best with **6, 9, 22** (Ideal for ethical, humanitarian ventures.)

Example: Sarah (Life Path 5) partnered with Tom (Life Path 8). Initially, Tom's love for structure clashed with Sarah's need for adventure. Once they divided roles—Sarah handling creativity, Tom managing finances—they found **business harmony** and scaled their startup **beyond expectations**.

How Successful Companies Unknowingly Follow Numerology Principles

Ever wonder why **some businesses seem to have an unstoppable energy** while others feel doomed from day one? Numerology often explains **why certain brands dominate their industries** without even realizing they align with powerful number vibrations.

Step 1: Calculate a Business Name's Numerology

1. Assign each letter in the business name a number using this chart:

Letters	A, J, S	B, K, T	C, L, U	D, M, V	E, N, W	F, O, X	G, P, Y	H, Q, Z	I, R
Numbers	1	2	3	4	5	6	7	8	9

2. Add up all the digits in the business name.
3. Reduce to a single digit (or Master Number 11, 22, 33).

Example: Apple Inc.

- A (1) + P (7) + P (7) + L (3) + E (5) = 23 → 2 + 3 = **5**
- **5** is the number of adaptability, communication, and constant reinvention. Apple perfectly aligns with this energetic vibration!

Business Name Numbers & Their Meanings

- **1** – Leadership, innovation (Tesla, Amazon)
- **2** – Balance, partnerships (Pepsi, Visa)
- **3** – Creativity, marketing (Disney, Instagram)
- **4** – Stability, trust (IBM, Home Depot)

- **5** – Change, adaptability (Apple, Facebook)
- **6** – Service, responsibility (Starbucks, FedEx)
- **7** – Knowledge, analysis (Google, Wikipedia)
- **8** – Power, wealth (Nike, Goldman Sachs)
- **9** – Humanitarianism, big-picture (Tesla, Patagonia)
- **Master Number 11** – Visionary (YouTube, Netflix)
- **Master Number 22** – Legacy builders (Microsoft, Ford)
- **Master Number 33** – Global impact (WWF, Red Cross)

Example: Elon Musk's **Tesla (Life Path 1)** thrives on **innovation and leadership**, making it a perfect match for numerology's energy of pioneering new industries.

The Best Numerology Numbers for Business Launch Dates

Just like you wouldn't get married on a bad numerology day (unless you enjoy emotional rollercoasters), launching a business on the wrong day can set you up for struggle from day one. The right timing can be the difference between **hitting the jackpot or barely keeping the lights on**.

- **Best Personal Days & Months to Launch a Business:**
  - **1 or 8** – Ideal for **bold, independent ventures and financial success.**
  - **3** – Great for creative businesses, media, and entertainment.
  - **5** – Perfect for fast-moving industries and tech startups.
  - **Master Number 22** – For **legacy-building, long-term success.**

Example: Amazon was founded in **July (7th month),** aligning with its **Life Path 7 energy** of deep analysis and knowledge. The company is obsessed with data, innovation, and AI—classic 7 traits.

Office & Business Address Numerology – Location Matters!

Ever walked into a business and **immediately felt its energy**? Turns out, your office address has a numerology vibration too. The **numbers in your business address can attract or repel financial success.**

How to Calculate Your Business Address Number

1. Take the street number of your office/building.

2. Add the digits together until you get a single digit (or Master Number 11, 22, 33).

Example: Google's headquarters is at **1600 Amphitheatre Parkway**:

- **1 + 6 + 0 + 0 = 7**
- **7 is the number of deep research, intelligence, and innovation.** No surprise Google dominates in knowledge-based services!

Best Address Numbers for Different Business Types

- **1** – Leadership, strong branding (Great for solo entrepreneurs, consulting firms)
- **3** – Creativity, communication (Great for media, entertainment, and marketing firms)
- **4** – Stability, structure (Ideal for banks, law firms, real estate offices)
- **5** – Change, high energy (Tech startups, travel agencies, social media firms)
- **8** – Money, power (Best for financial institutions, investment firms, and high-growth businesses)
- **Master Number 22** – Business legacy (Perfect for companies aiming for long-term global impact)

Hiring Employees & Team Dynamics Based on Numerology

Want to know why some teams are a **powerhouse of productivity** while others collapse under the weight of their own chaos? It might be their numerology mismatch.

How to Use Numerology in Hiring & Team Building

- **Life Path 1** – Best in leadership roles, but doesn't like micromanagement.
- **Life Path 3** – Marketing, PR, and creative positions—fantastic at making ideas **sound amazing.**
- **Life Path 4** – Operations, HR, and finance—**masters of structure and process.**
- **Life Path 5** – Sales, networking, and event planning—thrives in fast-paced environments.
- **Life Path 8** – Financial strategists, business growth specialists—**obsessed with money.**

Example: Sarah, a **Life Path 3**, was miserable in a finance role where she **had to follow strict rules all day**. When she switched to a marketing role, **her creativity exploded,** and she tripled her company's social media engagement. Right number, right job!

Business Cycles & Growth Based on Numerology Years

Just like people, **businesses go through Personal Year Cycles.** Knowing whether your business is in a **growth phase, transition year, or rebranding moment** can save you from making financial missteps.

How to Calculate Your Business Year Number

Add up the digits of the year your business was founded.

Reduce to a single digit (or Master Number 11, 22, 33).

Best Business Years for Growth & Expansion

- **1 Year** – Perfect for launching, rebranding, or starting fresh.
- **4 Year** – Ideal for **building solid foundations and fixing weak points.**
- **8 Year** – High-revenue year! Great for expansions, big investments.
- **9 Year** – Wrap-up year—**finish old projects, prepare for the next cycle.**

Example: A startup in a **9 Year** tried to expand but struggled with finances. They should have **waited until their 1 Year** for growth and **focused on clearing debts instead.** Timing matters!

The Role of Karmic Debt in Business (And How to Overcome It)

Ever feel like **your business is cursed** no matter what you do? If your company's numerology contains **Karmic Debt Numbers (13, 14, 16, 19),** you might be dealing with some past-life financial baggage.

What Karmic Debt Numbers Mean in Business

- **13** – Struggle, slow growth, lots of effort needed (requires discipline & persistence)
- **14** – Financial instability, unexpected losses (needs strong money management)

- **16** – Reputation issues, unexpected downfalls (transparency and ethics are key)
- **19** – Leadership struggles, power imbalances (avoid ego clashes in partnerships)

Example: A company with **Karmic Debt 16** constantly faced **scandals and lawsuits**. When they rebranded under a new name without a Karmic Debt Number, their **public perception improved almost overnight.**

Using Numerology to Build a Thriving Business

Numerology isn't about **letting numbers rule your life**—it's about **stacking the odds in your favor**. The most successful businesses unknowingly follow numerology principles, while **failing businesses often have misaligned numbers from the start**.

If you're launching a new venture, looking for a co-founder, or wondering why your brand isn't taking off, **checking your numerology could reveal exactly what needs to change**.

Because let's be honest—if **Fortune 500 companies are vibing with numerology (even unintentionally), why shouldn't you?**

Part 2
Timing & Market Cycles

Personal Timing – When to Invest, Save, or HoDL

Because Even Money Moves Have a Season

Ever feel like every financial decision you make is either **perfectly timed or a complete disaster**? Maybe you invested in crypto at its peak only to watch it nosedive, or you sold a stock **right before** it skyrocketed. Bad luck? Maybe. But more likely, you weren't **aligned with your numerology cycle**.

Numerology isn't just about **who you are**—it's about **when you should (or shouldn't) make financial moves**. And let's be honest: sometimes the best move is **not moving at all**. So, before you throw money at the stock market, buy a house, or start your dream business, let's figure out **when the universe is actually on your side.**

The Personal Year Cycle: Your Financial Forecast

Much like the **seasons of the year**, your Personal Year number dictates whether it's time to **plant financial seeds, grow your investments, or cash out and start fresh.** Understanding this cycle can keep you from making financial moves at the worst possible time (like investing in NFTs in a 9 Year—yikes).

What Each Personal Year Means for Your Money Moves

Personal Year 1 – The Financial Fresh Start

- **Best for:** Launching a business, starting a new investment plan, taking bold financial risks.
- **Avoid:** Sticking to old money habits—this year is all about reinvention.

Example: David used his **Personal Year 1** to launch an online coaching business. By the end of the year, he had a thriving six-figure income. Had he waited, the momentum wouldn't have been there.

Personal Year 2 – Slow & Steady Wins the Race

- **Best for:** Financial planning, partnerships, researching investments.
- **Avoid:** Rushing into major investments—this is a year for patience.

Example: Olivia wanted to buy a rental property but felt uneasy. Instead, she **spent the year researching** and found a much better deal in her **Personal Year 3**.

Personal Year 3 – The Creative Wealth-Building Year

- **Best for:** Monetizing hobbies, side hustles, marketing, expanding your brand.
- **Avoid: Overspending** on unnecessary luxuries (seriously, you don't need another vacation right now).

Example: Alex, a Life Path 3, launched a YouTube channel in his Personal Year 3. By the end of the year, he was making **passive income** from ad revenue.

Personal Year 4 – The Financial Stability Year

- **Best for:** Budgeting, long-term investments, saving, buying property.
- **Avoid:** Risky investments—this year favors **solid, structured money moves.**

Example: Mark used his **Personal Year 4** to max out his retirement accounts and purchase a rental property. Now, his future self is thanking him.

Personal Year 5 – The Wild Card Year

- **Best for:** Taking calculated financial risks, diversifying investments, exploring new opportunities.
- **Avoid:** Impulsive spending—this year **loves surprises (not always good ones).**

Example: Sarah invested in a **fast-growing startup** in her Personal Year 5. She made a huge return—but only because she researched it first. Her friend, who gambled on meme stocks, wasn't so lucky.

Personal Year 6 – The Financial Security Year

- **Best for:** Investing in home, family, and community wealth.
- **Avoid:** Neglecting personal financial goals by over-giving to others.

Example: Jake bought his first home in his **Personal Year 6**—a perfect move since this year supports **long-term stability.**

Personal Year 7 – The Research Year

- **Best for:** Learning, **analyzing markets**, setting up future investments.
- **Avoid:** Making impulsive financial decisions—this year is about **strategy, not action.**

Example: Michelle **almost** started a business in her **Personal Year 7**, but instead, she spent the year studying her industry. The next year, she launched successfully.

Personal Year 8 – The Wealth-Building Year

- **Best for:** High-stakes investments, career moves, and financial growth.
- **Avoid:** Playing small—this is your **power year.**

Example: Robert negotiated a major promotion and started **investing aggressively** in real estate. By the end of the year, he had doubled his income.

Personal Year 9 – The Year of Financial Completion

- **Best for:** Wrapping up old investments, clearing debt, cashing out.
- **Avoid:** Starting **anything new**—this year is about **closing cycles.**

Example: Lisa sold her **underperforming stocks** in her Personal Year 9 and reinvested in a **new strategy for her upcoming Year 1.**

Master Numbers & Personal Year Financial Timing

If you have a Master Number **(11, 22, or 33)**, congratulations—you have extra financial energy at play. These years bring **big shifts, breakthroughs, and heightened potential**—but also require discipline to **avoid burnout and financial missteps.**

Master Number 11 – The Visionary Financial Year

- **Best for:** Inspired financial decisions, starting passion-based businesses, networking.
- **Avoid:** Overanalyzing every move—**trust your intuition.**

Example: Rachel, a Master Number 11, launched a **coaching business** during her Personal Year 11 and found rapid success—once she stopped second-guessing herself.

Master Number 22 – The Legacy Wealth Year

- **Best for:** Building long-term investments, scaling businesses, and creating financial empires.

- **Avoid:** Getting lost in perfectionism—**execute your financial plans!**

Example: Steve, a Life Path 22, used his **Personal Year 22** to expand his real estate portfolio, securing generational wealth for his family.

Master Number 33 – The Philanthropy & Wealth Alignment Year

- **Best for:** Aligning money with purpose, impact investing, launching ethical businesses.
- **Avoid:** Giving too much—**balance giving with smart financial planning.**

Example: Monica, a Master Number 33, **started a non-profit with a sustainable revenue model** in her Personal Year 33, allowing her to make an impact without financial struggles.

Numerology & Economic Cycles – Do Market Trends Follow Numerology?

Ever notice that economic recessions, stock market crashes, and financial booms seem to happen in patterns? Spoiler alert: **they do.** And numerology just might be the secret indicator Wall Street hedge funds don't want you to know about.

Historical Market Events & Numerology

- **2008 Financial Crisis** (Global Year 1) – The market got **reset hard** (a very 1-Year move).
- **1929 Stock Market Crash** (Global Year 2) – A year of cooperation? Well, investors learned the hard way to be *very* cooperative with financial regulations after the Great Depression.
- **2020 Pandemic Crash** (Global Year 4) – Stability? More like chaos, but 4 does force long-term restructuring. And what did we get? A financial reset with a wave of **digital investments** and crypto explosions.

Moral of the story: If the entire **global economy listens to numerology (even unintentionally), maybe you should too.**

The Best Personal Year for Major Financial Moves (By Category)

So, when should you make those **big money moves**? Here's your cheat sheet:

- **Buying a Home: Personal Year 4 or 6** (Think long-term stability. Unless you enjoy foreclosure.)
- **Starting a Business: Personal Year 1 or 8** (Momentum and money energy are at their peak.)
- **Changing Careers: Personal Year 5 or 9** (Embrace change. Just don't get fired first.)

Example: Laura waited until her **Personal Year 6** to buy a home, and she locked in the **best deal of her life.** Had she done it in a **Personal Year 5**, she probably would've ended up **in a house that needed constant repairs and an exorcism.**

Combining Personal Year & Life Path for Even More Precision

If you really want to get advanced (or you just love overanalyzing everything like a Life Path 7), then let's add your **Life Path Number** to the mix. Because your **Personal Year** affects everyone differently depending on their core numerology.

How Different Life Paths React to Personal Year Cycles

- **Life Path 1 in a Personal Year 1?** Time to **dominate the game**. Launch that business!
- **Life Path 5 in a Personal Year 5?** Buckle up. It's gonna be a rollercoaster of opportunity (and chaos).
- **Life Path 9 in a Personal Year 9?** Get ready for **some deep reflection**—don't fight the endings, embrace them.

Example: Tom (Life Path 8) hit a **Personal Year 4** and thought it was time to **take big risks** in real estate. Bad move. 4 Years demand **caution, planning, and patience**—instead, he got stuck with a house that needed more repairs than his bank account could handle.

When NOT to Invest – The Numerology "Red Flag" Years

Everyone wants to know when to **strike gold**, but sometimes, the **best investment is the one you DON'T make.**

Personal Years That Are Financial Traps

- **Personal Year 7** – Great for research, terrible for action. Unless you enjoy losing money on impulse decisions.
- **Personal Year 9** – Endings, completions, and wrapping up cycles. Not the time to start a **brand-new investment venture.**

Example: Lisa ignored numerology and started a **business in her Personal Year 9**. One year later? Closed doors, financial losses, and a painful lesson. If she had waited for her **Personal Year 1**, she would've had **momentum working in her favor.**

Timing Your Financial Moves Like a Pro

If you've ever wondered why some financial decisions feel **effortless while others crash and burn**, it's likely because you were **aligned (or misaligned) with your numerology cycle**.

Before you dive into your next investment, take a moment to **check your Personal Year**—because let's face it, making smart money moves is hard enough without fighting against the universe.

Market Cycles & Numerology Timing – Predicting Trends

Can Numerology Predict Bull & Bear Markets? (And Save You from Bad Financial Decisions?)

If you've ever bought a stock or crypto **at the absolute peak** and then watched it nosedive faster than your motivation at a Monday morning meeting, you're not alone. But what if I told you that **market cycles** aren't just random fluctuations—numerology might actually be one of the missing puzzle pieces?

Yes, Wall Street traders will call it **"data-driven forecasting,"** and economists will say **"market sentiment"**—but at the end of the day, financial trends follow patterns. And **numerology is all about patterns.**

So, instead of relying on **financial "gurus" who conveniently disappear when the market crashes**, let's use numerology to help you time your moves like a pro (or at least avoid going broke).

The Market's Numerology Cycles – The Hidden Math Behind Booms & Busts

Just like you have **Personal Years**, the global economy also experiences **numerology cycles** that influence **financial booms, recessions, and crashes.** Think of these cycles as the **unseen forces shaping market behavior.**

How to Calculate the Market's Global Year Number

1. Take the **current year** and add up all the digits.
2. Reduce to a single digit (unless it's a Master Number 11, 22, or 33).

Example: Global Year for 2025

- 2 + 0 + 2 + 5 = **9**
- **2025 is a Global Year 9 – A year of endings, restructuring, and financial shake-ups.** (Translation: If you're riding a bull market in Year 8, you might want to cash out before Year 9 pulls the rug.)

Now, let's see how these global cycles affect market trends.

Bull vs. Bear Markets – When Numerology Says to Go All In or Sit Tight

Markets fluctuate between **bull runs (when prices surge) and bear markets (when everything tanks and investors panic).** What if I told you numerology could help you see these shifts coming?

How Each Global Year Affects the Market

- **Global Year 1 – New financial cycles begin.** Innovations, startups, and fresh market trends emerge. Great for launching businesses and investing in new industries.
- **Global Year 2 – Market consolidation.** Mergers, partnerships, and slower growth. A year to **wait and observe** before making big moves.

- **Global Year 3 – Expansion & hype.** Speculation increases, and the media hypes up stocks and crypto. Be cautious of **bubble formations.**
- **Global Year 4 – Reality check.** Market corrections, government regulations, and financial discipline take center stage.
- **Global Year 5 – Volatility!** Sudden spikes and dips. A great year for **trading** but a nightmare for long-term stability.
- **Global Year 6 – Recovery & stabilization.** Ideal for real estate and infrastructure investments.
- **Global Year 7 – Economic reflection & research.** A quiet year where hidden market trends start forming.
- **Global Year 8 – Wealth-building & major financial shifts.** This is the year **big money is made or lost.**
- **Global Year 9 – End of cycles.** Expect **major crashes, recessions, or financial resets.** If you didn't cash out in Year 8, buckle up.
- **Master Number 11 – Financial awakenings.** A year where **new financial paradigms emerge, visionary ideas take hold, and speculative investments can turn into long-term winners.**
- **Master Number 22 – Building financial empires.** This is the year when **massive institutions, governments, and major corporations make bold moves that reshape industries.** Excellent for long-term investments.
- **Master Number 33 – Global wealth redistribution.** A year that focuses on **philanthropy, economic balance, and large-scale financial shifts that impact global economies.** Great for ethical investing and social enterprise growth.

Example: The **Great Depression began in 1929 (Global Year 2),** a year of economic hesitation and uncertainty. The **2008 financial crisis hit in a Global Year 1**, signaling the start of a **new (and painful) financial cycle.** Coincidence? Probably not.

Timing Major Financial Events & Market Crashes

If numerology can **predict cycles**, can it also **help you avoid financial wipeouts?** Yes—if you know when to hold 'em and when to fold 'em.

Key Numerology Red Flags for Market Crashes

- **Personal Year 9 + Global Year 9:** If both your personal cycle and the global cycle are at an end, **this is NOT the time to YOLO into high-risk investments.**

- **Global Year 5:** Wild fluctuations. If you love gambling, enjoy the ride, but don't expect stability.
- **Global Year 7:** Hidden cracks in the system. Everything looks fine—until it's not.

Example: Jake ignored numerology and went **all-in on speculative stocks during a Global Year 9.** Six months later, he watched his portfolio collapse like a bad first date. Meanwhile, Sarah cashed out **right before** the downturn, because she followed numerology cycles.

Crypto, Forex, and Alternative Investments – What Numerology Says

If you think **crypto, forex, and speculative trading** operate outside of numerology, think again. **They follow cycles too.**

When to Enter & Exit Crypto Based on Numerology

- **Year 1 or 8:** Ideal for new blockchain projects and major market moves.
- **Year 3 or 5:** Expect hype-driven surges (and crashes right after).
- **Year 9:** If a coin is already peaking, consider taking profits before the cycle resets.

Example: Bitcoin peaked in late **2017 (Global Year 1)**, before **crashing in 2018 (Global Year 2)**—a classic example of numerology cycles in action. Seriously an 84% loss in one year and rally back 3,400% a couple years later from the low in 2018.

The Role of Numerology in Economic Bubbles & Crashes

Ever noticed how financial bubbles inflate with unstoppable optimism, only to burst in spectacular fashion? Numerology has a way of **predicting when the party is about to end**—and no, you don't need an MBA to see the signs.

- **Years 3 and 5** – These years bring **irrational exuberance** (think dot-com stocks and crypto bull runs). Everyone is throwing money at shiny new assets.
- **Years 7 and 9** – The financial equivalent of a hangover. Cracks appear, and by Year 9, it's **game over for overhyped investments**.

Example: The **2008 financial crisis (Global Year 1)** followed a **hype-driven real estate boom** in Global Years 3 and 5 (2006-2007). If investors had checked their numerology, they could've seen the impending crash.

Historical Stock Market Trends & Numerology Cycles

Let's play a game called "Was That a Coincidence, or Numerology at Work?" Here are some of the biggest financial events in history and their Global Year numbers:

- **Black Monday (1987, Global Year 7):** A year of **hidden problems** suddenly coming to light.
- **Dot-Com Bubble Burst (2000, Global Year 2):** A year of financial **reevaluation**—investors realized their "sure bets" were just **bad ideas with good marketing.**
- **COVID-19 Crash (2020, Global Year 4):** A correction year that shook the world economy into **financial lockdown mode.**

See the trend? Numerology isn't magic—it's just **patterns that repeat.**

How Numerology Aligns with Government & Central Bank Decisions

The Federal Reserve and global governments don't openly **consult numerology** before adjusting interest rates (or do they? 👀), but major economic policies tend to align with numerology cycles anyway.

- **Global Year 4 or 6:** Expect economic stimulus plans, infrastructure spending, and stabilization efforts.
- **Global Year 8:** Central banks tighten monetary policies, leading to wealth redistribution.
- **Global Year 9:** Economic resets—often **big market crashes** or recessions.

Example: In **Global Year 4 (2020),** governments worldwide **implemented financial stimulus packages** to stabilize economies. **Coincidence? Probably not.**

How to Use Numerology to Build a Recession-Proof Investment Strategy

If you want to **stay ahead of market crashes and recessions**, numerology can act as your **financial compass.**

Wealth Strategies for Each Numerology Cycle

- **Years 1 & 2:** Start new investments and position yourself for growth.
- **Years 3 & 5:** Ride the market's momentum—but don't hold too long.
- **Years 7 & 9:** Time to **sell off risky assets and protect your wealth.**

Example: Investors who pulled out before **Global Year 9 (2008)** saved themselves from the real estate collapse. Those who ignored the cycle? Well... let's just say **they learned a painful lesson.**

Business & Corporate Numerology: How Companies Time Their Moves

Big corporations and hedge funds **might not admit it**, but they time their major financial moves **in alignment with numerology trends** (even if unknowingly).

- **IPO Launches:** Many major companies **go public in Global Year 1 or 8** for maximum financial impact.
- **Mergers & Acquisitions:** Companies consolidate in **Global Years 2 and 6** when partnerships thrive.
- **Rebrands & Restructuring:** Happens in **Global Year 9**, when businesses cut losses and prepare for a new cycle.

Example: Amazon and Apple have strategically expanded their businesses **during Global Year 8 cycles**, aligning with peak financial energy for **maximum profit.**

Using Numerology to Time Your Market Moves

The stock market, crypto, real estate, and global finance aren't just **chaotic forces**—they follow cycles, patterns, and (if you're paying attention) **numerology trends.**

Before you **panic-buy at the top or sell at the bottom,** check where we are in the global cycle. Numerology isn't a crystal ball, but it **can** give you an edge over investors who are just winging it.

Because let's be real—if hedge funds and billionaires secretly use cycles to time their investments, why shouldn't you?

Home & Real Estate Numerology – Investing in Property

Your Home's Numerology: More Than Just an Address

You might think that a house is just a house—four walls, a roof, and a mortgage that haunts you for decades. But **what if your home's address number actually influences your financial success?** Numerology suggests that your **house number carries an energy** that affects everything from your wealth-building potential to how harmonious your home life is.

So, before you blame your bad luck on the economy, maybe it's time to **check your address.**

How to Calculate Your Home's Numerology Number

Before you panic-sell your house because of a "bad" number, let's break it down:

1. Take the digits of your **house or apartment number** (ignore street names).
2. Add them together until you get a **single digit or Master Number** (11, 22, 33).

Example: If you live at **742 Maple Street**:

- 7 + 4 + 2 = **13** → 1 + 3 = **4**
- Your home is a **4-energy house** (great for stability and hard work, but maybe a little rigid).

If you live in **Apartment #27**:

- 2 + 7 = **9** → Your personal living space carries a **9-energy**, which is great for compassion and wisdom but might not be ideal for material wealth.

What Your Home's Number Says About Wealth & Success

Each home number has a **different energy**—some attract abundance, while others make saving money harder than resisting a Black Friday sale.

House Numbers & Their Financial Impact

- **1:** Great for independence and entrepreneurial ventures, but can feel isolating.
- **2:** Encourages partnerships, family stability, and shared wealth.
- **3:** Boosts creativity and social opportunities, but can lead to overspending.
- **4:** Solid for financial stability and long-term investments (but prepare for slow, steady growth).
- **5:** A wild card—great for business expansion but risky for long-term stability.
- **6:** Excellent for family wealth-building, real estate investments, and stability.
- **7:** A spiritual retreat—good for reflection, not necessarily financial gains.
- **8:** The **ultimate wealth-building number**—ideal for high earners and business owners.
- **9:** Encourages generosity and humanitarian efforts, but might not be ideal for wealth accumulation.
- **Master Number 11:** Inspires visionary success but requires strong focus.

- **Master Number 22:** The ultimate **wealth builder**—great for real estate moguls and empire-building.
- **Master Number 33:** A home with purpose—great for community projects and philanthropic success.

Example: Megan was struggling financially until she moved into a home with an **8-energy address**. Within two years, her income tripled, and she finally felt financially secure. Coincidence? Maybe. But numerology suggests **her house was vibing with wealth energy.**

Best Years to Buy, Sell, or Hold Property (Based on Numerology)

If you're thinking about buying, selling, or investing in real estate, **timing is everything.** Not just in terms of interest rates and market conditions—but also your **Personal Year Number.**

How to Calculate Your Personal Year Number

1. Add your **birth month** + **birth day** + **current year**.
2. Reduce to a single digit (or Master Number 11, 22, 33).

Example: If you were born on **April 15** and it's **2025**:

- 4 + 1 + 5 + 2 + 0 + 2 + 5 = **19** → 1 + 9 = **10** → 1 + 0 = **1**
- You're in a **Personal Year 1**—great for starting new things, including buying property!

Best Personal Years for Real Estate Moves

- **Personal Year 1:** Great for buying your first home or investment property.
- **Personal Year 2:** Best for **partnership-based investments** (but not rushing solo deals).
- **Personal Year 3:** A good time to renovate or **flip a property** for profit.
- **Personal Year 4:** Stability year—ideal for **long-term real estate investments.**
- **Personal Year 5:** Be cautious! Markets may fluctuate wildly.
- **Personal Year 6:** Best year for buying a family home or expanding real estate holdings.
- **Personal Year 7:** A research year—learn about investing but hold off on major purchases.

- **Personal Year 8: The best year for big real estate deals.** Money energy is high.
- **Personal Year 9:** Time to **sell** or wrap up property-related affairs.
- **Master Number 11:** Ideal for visionary investments, but requires intuition and patience.
- **Master Number 22: The ultimate year for real estate wealth-building.**
- **Master Number 33:** Best for **community housing projects or real estate tied to philanthropy.**

Example: Ben bought his first home in his **Personal Year 8**—the deal was seamless, and within two years, his property value skyrocketed. Meanwhile, his friend Joe bought in a **Personal Year 5** and faced endless market fluctuations. **Moral of the story: Timing matters!**

Using Numerology to Choose Profitable Real Estate Investments

So, now that you know **timing and house numbers matter**, how do you actually **apply numerology to real estate investments?**

Checklist for Profitable Numerology-Based Investing

- **Check the address number** – Aim for 6, 8, or 22 for financial growth.
- **Time your purchase wisely** – Personal Year 1, 4, 6, or 8 are best.
- **Align with your Life Path** – If you're a Life Path 4 or 8, real estate is naturally in your wealth-building toolkit.
- **Avoid Karmic Debt Numbers (13, 14, 16, 19)** – These homes may bring unexpected challenges or financial instability.

Example: Lisa, a Life Path 8, specifically sought out **8-energy properties** and bought during her **Personal Year 4**. Within three years, her real estate investments had doubled in value. **She played the numerology game and won.**

Karmic Debt in Real Estate – Avoiding Problem Properties

Ever moved into a house and suddenly **everything in life started going downhill**? Maybe the plumbing burst, your finances took a nosedive, or your neighbor turned out to be a banshee in disguise. Welcome to the world of **Karmic Debt Numbers in real estate.**

Certain house numbers—**13, 14, 16, and 19**—carry **Karmic Debt energy**, meaning they come with lessons and challenges. These properties tend to have **unexpected repairs, legal issues, and financial setbacks.**

How to Spot & Avoid Karmic Debt Properties

- **Check the address number**—if it adds up to 13, 14, 16, or 19, proceed with caution.
- If you MUST live in one, **balance the energy with personal numerology strategies** (or maybe just stockpile some extra home insurance).

Example: Josh moved into a house with a **16-energy address**. Within six months:

- The **roof caved in**.
- The **HVAC system died in mid-July**.
- His **cat mysteriously disappeared** (it eventually came back, but still—suspicious).

Lesson learned: **Check the numerology first.**

Feng Shui & Numerology – Double the Energy Alignment

If you really want to **supercharge** your home's wealth energy, combining **numerology with Feng Shui** is like giving your finances a cosmic-level power boost.

How to Align Numerology & Feng Shui for Maximum Prosperity

- **House Number 8?** Fantastic! Now place a **Feng Shui wealth bowl** in your prosperity corner.
- **Living in a 4-house (slow growth)?** Add **red accents** to fire up the energy.
- **House Number 7 (spiritual retreat)?** Perfect if you want peace, but not great for material wealth—add some metal elements for financial grounding.

Example: Jennifer moved into an **8-energy house** and used Feng Shui tactics—within a year, her **business doubled in revenue**. Coincidence? Maybe. But numerology says otherwise.

Commercial Real Estate & Business Locations – Picking Profitable Spaces

Your **business address matters too**—because if you're opening a **storefront, office, or investment property**, the number can **influence foot traffic, sales, and long-term success.**

Best Numerology Numbers for Business Locations

- **1** – Best for solo entrepreneurs, startups, and independent ventures.
- **5** – Perfect for fast-paced businesses (tech, media, restaurants, travel agencies).
- **8** – The **wealth magnet**—ideal for banks, investment firms, and high-profit businesses.
- **22** – Best for large-scale enterprises and corporate headquarters.

Example: A restaurant in a **5-energy location** thrived with a constant stream of customers. Meanwhile, a competing restaurant down the block (in a 7-energy location) struggled with foot traffic. **Numerology wins again!**

House Flipping & Investment Strategies Using Numerology

If you're into **flipping houses or investing in rental properties**, numerology can help you **choose profitable locations, perfect your timing, and sell fast.**

Best Years to Flip Houses & Invest

- **Personal Year 1, 3, 4, or 8** – Great for property investments and flipping.
- **Personal Year 9** – NOT the year to start flipping. Sell instead.

How to Match a Home's Numerology to the Buyer

- Selling a house? **Market it to a buyer whose Life Path matches the house number.**
- Example: An **8-energy home** is great for an **entrepreneur or business mogul**.

Example: Mark, a real estate investor, only flipped houses with **6 or 8-energy addresses**. His homes **sold faster and at higher prices** compared to investors dealing with "unlucky" numbers. **Coincidence? Maybe. But Mark doesn't take chances.**

Numerology & Mortgage/Loan Success – Timing Your Approval Process

Timing matters when it comes to **securing funding for a home or investment property**. If you apply for a mortgage or loan in the **wrong Personal Year**, you might hit unnecessary roadblocks.

Best Personal Years for Mortgage Approvals & Home Loans

- **Personal Year 1 or 8** – Ideal for securing funding and making major financial moves.
- **Personal Year 4 or 6** – Great for **long-term property investments**.
- **Personal Year 5** – Be cautious! Unexpected changes could impact financial stability.

Example: Lisa applied for a mortgage in her **Personal Year 6** and got approved **instantly**. Meanwhile, Tom applied in his **Personal Year 7** and spent **months dealing with unnecessary paperwork.**

Hacking Your House Number – Fixing a 'Bad' Address

So, you ran the numbers, and your house has an energy that's **less than ideal** for financial success. Maybe you're stuck with a **karmic debt house**, or your address number is just too unpredictable for your taste.

The good news? **You don't have to move—just hack the energy!**

How to Fix a Bad House Number with Numerology

- **Add a Number** – If your house number adds up to a 4 (slow growth), place a small number **on your door or mailbox** that shifts the energy. For example, if your home adds up to a 4, adding a discreet "1" somewhere nearby could turn it into a 5 (bringing more flexibility and financial movement).
- **Use Color Therapy** – Certain colors can **enhance or neutralize numerology energy.** Got a house with a 7-energy (which is great for wisdom but not for wealth)? Paint the **front door red** or add gold accents to attract financial success.
- **Leverage Symbols & Objects** – Placing **wealth symbols like lucky coins, money trees, or Feng Shui prosperity items** near the entrance can override negative financial energy.
- **Reinforce the Desired Energy** – If your house number is an 8 (already great for wealth), keep the vibe strong by using **metallic tones, strong lighting, and a clear, well-maintained entryway.**

Example: Emily's home had a **13-energy address**, which screamed **karmic debt** (aka unexpected financial headaches). Instead of moving, she **added a "9" plaque next to the door** to shift the energy. Within months, her financial situation **stabilized**, and she landed a better job. Coincidence? Maybe. But it worked.

Your House Number & Real Estate Wealth

If you've ever felt like a house just **"felt right"** (or terribly wrong), numerology might explain why. Whether you're buying your dream home or expanding your investment portfolio, knowing how **numbers influence real estate** could be the **missing financial strategy you never knew you needed.**

Because let's face it—if numbers run the economy, why wouldn't they also run real estate?

Passive Income, Wealth Protection & Future-Proofing

Because Your Money Should Work Harder Than You Do

Let's be honest—if making money meant **working non-stop for 40 years** only to retire on a fixed income and a prayer, we'd all collectively throw in the towel. Luckily, **passive income exists**, and numerology can actually tell you **the best ways to build, protect, and sustain wealth** without losing sleep over every market dip.

Passive income isn't just about **collecting rent checks, dividend payouts, or running an online business while lounging on a beach**—it's about aligning with **the right numerology cycles** to ensure your money flows effortlessly instead of disappearing faster than your paycheck on payday.

So let's break it down: how can **numbers help you build long-term wealth, minimize risk, and ensure financial security even when the economy is throwing tantrums?**

How Numerology Aligns with Passive Income Strategies

Not all passive income strategies **work for everyone**—what's perfect for one person might be **a financial disaster for another.** That's where numerology comes in.

Aligning Passive Income with Your Life Path Number

- **Life Path 1** – Best for solo ventures like self-publishing, digital products, and personal brand businesses.
- **Life Path 2** – Partnership-based passive income (joint real estate, affiliate marketing, or royalties from co-created work).
- **Life Path 3** – Creative income streams (YouTube, blogging, content licensing, or monetized art).
- **Life Path 4** – Real estate investments, dividend stocks, and long-term business models.
- **Life Path 5** – High-risk, high-reward income (crypto staking, trading bots, unconventional investments).
- **Life Path 6** – Passive income that benefits communities (nonprofits, property rentals, ethical investments).
- **Life Path 7** – Research-heavy passive streams (writing, intellectual property, data-driven investments).
- **Life Path 8** – The ultimate wealth-builders: real estate moguls, stock investors, and business owners.
- **Life Path 9** – Passive income with purpose (philanthropic funds, impact investing, trust funds).
- **Master Number 11** – Innovative financial models (patents, tech investments, visionary ventures).
- **Master Number 22** – Empire-building passive income (corporate real estate, financial portfolios, large-scale licensing deals).
- **Master Number 33** – Wealth that creates impact (charitable foundations, social enterprises, sustainable investing).

Example: Tim, a **Life Path 4**, originally tried flipping NFTs and crypto trading but failed miserably. After shifting to **real estate rentals and long-term index funds** (which matched his stable, structured energy), he started seeing **consistent passive income without the stress.**

Best Numerology Years for Wealth Building & Passive Income Expansion

Your **Personal Year Number** also determines whether it's the right time to **expand your income streams, reinvest, or sit tight and let your money grow.**

Best Years to Focus on Passive Income

- **Personal Year 1:** New financial ventures and income streams.
- **Personal Year 4:** Long-term investment foundations.
- **Personal Year 6:** Real estate and community-driven wealth.
- **Personal Year 8:** Maximum wealth expansion—**the best year to build financial empires!**
- **Master Number 22:** The **ultimate** passive income year—think major wealth accumulation.

Years to Be Cautious

- **Personal Year 5:** High volatility—avoid reckless financial decisions.
- **Personal Year 7:** A research year—learn, but don't take big risks.
- **Personal Year 9:** Completion year—time to exit underperforming investments.

Example: Lisa tried launching **a rental property business in a Personal Year 9** and lost money when the housing market shifted. If she had waited until **her Personal Year 1**, she would have entered at a **perfect cycle for expansion.**

Wealth Protection & Risk Management – Not Losing Your Hard-Earned Money

Making money is **only half the battle—keeping it is the real challenge.** One market crash, economic downturn, or bad investment, and you could be watching your wealth disappear faster than an influencer's apology video.

Numerology's Guide to Smart Wealth Protection

- **Personal Year 4:** Best time for financial audits and long-term planning.
- **Personal Year 8:** Protect assets while expanding wealth.
- **Master Number 22:** Legacy wealth-building—think trusts, wills, and real estate portfolios.

Strategies to Secure Wealth Using Numerology

- **Diversification** – Spread your investments **across stable numerology-driven assets**.
- **Timing major financial moves** – Avoid signing risky contracts in a **Personal Year 5 or 7**.
- **Wealth energy shifts** – Use **Feng Shui, numerology, and financial strategies** to maintain a steady flow.

Example: Mark, a **Life Path 8**, went all-in on a **high-risk business venture in a Personal Year 5**—and it **collapsed within months.** Had he waited until **a Personal Year 8**, he could've made a fortune instead of a cautionary tale.

Future-Proofing Your Wealth with Numerology

Future-proofing wealth isn't just about **making money now—it's about ensuring you're financially stable in every cycle.**

Best Future-Proofing Strategies Based on Numerology

- **Aligning investments with Global Years** – Think of how major economic events align with numerology.
- **Estate planning in Year 4, 6, or 8** – Protect your assets for the long haul.
- **Expanding during numerology-aligned years** – Don't push expansion during a Year 7 or 9.

Example: Sophia built her **investment portfolio strategically using numerology**, expanding only in **Global Years 1 and 8**. Over time, her wealth stayed **secure through market crashes and recessions.**

Karmic Debt & Financial Lessons – Avoiding Wealth Traps

Just like bad relationships, **money also carries karmic debt.** If you've been experiencing **one financial disaster after another**, you might be carrying **Karmic Debt Numbers (13, 14, 16, 19).** These numbers indicate that **you're here to learn a financial lesson—probably the hard way.**

How to Break Free from Karmic Financial Cycles

- **13:** Hard work is required—there's no easy money. Learn **discipline, patience, and structure.**
- **14:** Stop the **impulsive spending and unstable investments**—find balance in financial decisions.
- **16:** Get out of your own way—your ego could be **sabotaging long-term success.**
- **19:** You must stand on your own feet—**avoid financial dependency and take responsibility.**

Example: Paul, a **Karmic 16**, kept losing money in get-rich-quick schemes. The moment he **focused on sustainable, long-term investments**, his wealth stopped vanishing into thin air.

Passive Income & The Energy of Numbers – Picking Wealth-Friendly Digits

If numbers influence everything, wouldn't it make sense that **your bank account number, investment accounts, and even business financials should align with wealth energy?**

Numbers That Support Wealth Growth

- **6:** Financial stability and wealth tied to home, family, and community.
- **8:** The ultimate number for **abundance, financial success, and high-level investments.**
- **22:** Ideal for **legacy wealth, generational fortune, and empire-building.**

Numbers That Can Sabotage Wealth

- **5:** High financial fluctuations—great for traders, but not for stable growth.
- **7:** Best for wisdom-based investments (education, research) but **not for material gains.**
- **Karmic Debt Numbers:** May indicate **financial struggles until lessons are learned.**

Example: Rachel had a bank account that added to **5** (chaotic energy). After switching to an account number that totaled **8,** her money habits improved, she saved more, and new opportunities arrived effortlessly.

Financial Minimalism – Cutting Unnecessary Money Leaks

If you make **good money but always feel broke**, congratulations—you may be leaking wealth without realizing it. Numerology can help identify **spending patterns** that need correction.

Using Numerology to Fix Financial Leaks

- **Life Path 3 & 5:** Prone to overspending—track finances more aggressively.
- **Personal Year 5:** Watch out for **impulsive financial decisions.**
- **Home or Business Number 4:** You might be holding onto outdated financial strategies—time for a reassessment.

Example: Sarah realized she was **spending on trends instead of real investments**. After aligning her budget with numerology, she doubled her savings in just a year.

The Numerology of Taxes – Timing Tax Moves with Your Personal Year

Nobody loves **tax season,** but with numerology, you can **at least avoid the worst timing for financial filings and audits.**

Best Years to Review & Optimize Tax Strategies

- **Year 4, 6, or 8:** Great for structuring tax-efficient investments, estate planning, and long-term strategies.

Years to Avoid Big Tax Moves

- **Year 5:** Too much instability—unexpected changes in laws or financial standing.
- **Year 7:** Investigation-heavy year—**don't give tax authorities a reason to dig deeper.**
- **Year 9:** A completion year—**not ideal for launching new tax strategies.**

Example: Michael did a **full tax audit during a Personal Year 4** and legally saved thousands by restructuring his investments.

Numerology & Generational Wealth – Teaching Financial Wisdom to the Next Generation

Wealth isn't just about **how much money you make**—it's also about **how well you pass down financial knowledge.**

Using Numerology for Generational Wealth Planning

- **Best Personal Years to set up trusts, wills, and family investments:** Year **4, 6, or 8**.
- **Choosing numerology-aligned assets** to ensure **sustained growth**.
- **Teaching your kids numerology-based financial habits** so they don't repeat common mistakes.

Example: Instead of just leaving money behind, Olivia taught her kids **how to invest, manage wealth, and use numerology cycles for financial success.** As a result, her children were already making **smarter money moves than most adults.**

Make Your Money Work for You

Numerology isn't just about **timing financial moves**—it's about building **long-term, sustainable wealth** that thrives in any market. The key is knowing **when to invest, when to wait, and how to protect your money from disappearing faster than a bad investment tip on Reddit.**

Because let's face it—**the wealthiest people aren't just working harder, they're working smarter.** And numerology might just be their **secret financial weapon.**

Giving Back – Philanthropy, Impact & Numerology

How to Give Back Without Going Broke (Or Becoming a Saint)

You've built wealth, or at least you're on your way—congratulations! But before you go **full Scrooge McDuck**, hoarding gold coins in a vault, let's talk about **giving back**.

Charitable giving isn't just about **feeling good or looking generous on social media**—it's also about **aligning with the cycles of abundance** so that your generosity **expands your wealth instead of depleting it.** And yes, numerology plays a part in **when, how, and where you give.**

If done correctly, philanthropy can be **a financial strategy, a legacy-building move, and a way to unlock higher energy flows of wealth.** But if done incorrectly, well... let's just say you'll end up with **empty pockets and a halo you didn't ask for.**

Aligning Charitable Giving with Numerology Cycles

Before you **throw money at random causes** and hope for good karma, consider that numerology can help you **time your giving for maximum impact**—on both the cause and your finances.

Best Personal Years for Giving Back

- **Personal Year 6:** The ultimate year of service. Giving back in this year strengthens relationships, builds goodwill, and even attracts unexpected financial blessings.
- **Personal Year 9:** The "completion year"—a time to **wrap up financial cycles and give to causes that support personal or global transformation.**
- **Master Number 33 Year:** A year of **high-impact giving**—this is when your philanthropy can change lives (and possibly history).

When to Be Cautious About Giving

- **Personal Year 1:** Focus on building your financial foundation first.
- **Personal Year 5:** Too much unpredictability—watch your budget before making large charitable commitments.

Example: Jake donated a large sum in a **Personal Year 9**, just before selling a business. That donation not only gave him **a huge tax deduction**, but it also aligned with his **closing financial cycles, opening doors for a new investment.**

How Much Should You Give? Numerology Has an Answer

Philanthropy isn't about going broke—it's about **giving strategically** so that your generosity **creates more wealth and goodwill.**

Using Numerology to Pick Your Giving Percentage

- **6% (Balance & Harmony):** A great percentage for consistent, sustainable giving.

- **8% (Wealth Activation):** Aligns with financial abundance and attracts prosperity.
- **9% (Completion & Universal Good):** Ideal for those wrapping up financial cycles or giving in honor of past success.
- **Master Number 22% (Legacy Giving):** For those looking to **fund major initiatives** or create lasting charitable institutions.

Example: Lisa structured her business to **donate 8% of annual profits**—not only did her company thrive, but the positive energy of her philanthropy also **attracted new clients and opportunities.**

Creating a Legacy of Wealth & Contribution

Want to make sure your impact lasts **longer than a trendy donation challenge?** Numerology can help you align with **legacy-building giving.**

Best Numerology Numbers for Lasting Impact

- **Life Path 6 & 9:** Natural givers who should focus on sustainable philanthropy.
- **Master Number 22 & 33:** Best suited for large-scale charitable ventures and legacy projects.
- **Home/Business Address Numbers 6, 8, or 9:** Living or working in spaces with these numerology energies enhances **philanthropic success.**

Example: Instead of writing a **one-time check**, David (a Life Path 9) created a **scholarship fund in alignment with his numerology cycles.** That fund continued to grow, benefiting students **long after he retired.**

Using Numerology to Choose the Right Causes

Giving is great, but **not all causes align with your numerology strengths.** Choose where you donate based on your Life Path, Personal Year, and financial cycles.

Best Causes Based on Numerology

- **Life Path 1:** Entrepreneurship, leadership mentorship programs.
- **Life Path 3:** Arts, creative education, youth initiatives.
- **Life Path 6:** Family, community welfare, housing programs.
- **Life Path 8:** Wealth-building initiatives and financial literacy programs.

- **Master Number 11:** Spiritual, visionary, and consciousness-based charities.
- **Master Number 22:** Large-scale infrastructure, education, and medical advancement projects.
- **Master Number 33:** Humanitarian causes, global relief efforts.

Example: Susan (Life Path 3) realized that every time she donated to **creative arts programs**, her business **experienced unexpected growth**—it turns out she was fueling **her own life path energy** through giving.

The Numerology of Giving Dates – When to Make Charitable Contributions

Timing matters, even in giving. Choosing **the right numerology dates** to donate can **enhance your financial prosperity** and ensure your gifts **create maximum impact.**

Best Days to Donate

- **6th, 9th, or 22nd of the month** – These dates align with humanitarian impact and wealth expansion.
- **Days that reduce to 8 (Wealth Energy)** – Great for activating financial abundance while giving.
- **Personal Day 6 or 9** – Perfect for charitable contributions.

Example: Mark planned his **largest annual donation on the 22nd of the month** during a **Personal Year 6**—not only did his business flourish after, but **his tax deduction was massive.**

The Karma of Money – Why Giving Unlocks More Wealth

Ever notice how **the wealthiest people are also major philanthropists**? It's not just good PR—**giving back creates a cycle of abundance.** Numerology suggests that when you **share your wealth in alignment with universal energy**, it **amplifies your prosperity** instead of draining it.

Why Giving Attracts More Wealth

- **Money is energy**—when it circulates with purpose, it returns multiplied.
- **Numerology cycles show** that certain years and numbers trigger expansive wealth **when generosity is involved.**

Example: Bill donated **millions during a Personal Year 9** (completion) and saw **his business profits skyrocket the next year. Coincidence? Maybe not.**

Numerology & Tax Benefits – Giving Smart, Not Just Generous

If you're going to **give back, do it with financial intelligence.**

Best Numerology Years for Tax-Deductible Donations

- **Year 6:** Ideal for structured giving.
- **Year 8:** High financial growth = high tax benefits.
- **Year 9:** Perfect for making final charitable contributions before a new cycle.

Example: Lisa **timed her charitable donations in a Personal Year 8**, reducing her taxable income while supporting her favorite causes.

Micro vs. Macro Philanthropy – What's Your Numerology-Driven Style?

Some people thrive on **big, legacy donations**, while others make **small, consistent contributions.** Numerology helps you **determine your ideal giving approach.**

Life Path-Giving Styles

- **1s & 8s:** Big, bold, and public giving (charity foundations, grants).
- **3s & 6s:** Community-driven giving (education, social programs).
- **9s & Master Numbers:** Humanitarian-focused giving (global relief, social justice).

Example: Olivia, a **Life Path 6**, focused on **local housing charities** instead of global organizations—resulting in more **impactful, aligned giving.**

Philanthropy & Business Growth – How Giving Back Attracts Success

Many successful businesses **incorporate charitable giving into their financial strategy.** Numerology shows that when businesses **give in aligned years**, they often experience **growth, customer loyalty, and unexpected new opportunities.**

Best Years for Businesses to Donate

- **Business Year 6:** Strong for ethical business models.
- **Business Year 8:** Great for **expansion-driven philanthropy.**
- **Business Year 9:** Closing cycles with impactful giving.

Example: A restaurant owner in a **Business Year 6** donated meals during a crisis—and **ended up attracting more customers and media coverage than ever before.**

Numerology & Legacy Projects – Building a Name That Lasts Beyond You

Want to **create a lasting foundation**? Numerology can help structure **long-term giving plans.**

Best Numerology Numbers for Legacy-Based Philanthropy

- **Master Number 22:** Best for large-scale projects (universities, hospitals).
- **Master Number 33:** Humanitarian efforts that last generations.
- **Life Path 9:** Perfect for global initiatives and lifelong charitable work.

Example: John (Master Number 22) structured **a trust that funds medical research**, ensuring his wealth benefits others **for generations.**

Giving & Receiving in Balance

Philanthropy isn't about **giving everything away and hoping for the best.** It's about creating **a cycle of wealth and impact**—when you align your giving with numerology, you ensure that **your generosity not only helps others but also fuels your financial success.**

So, the next time you reach for your wallet, ask yourself: **"Is this donation numerologically aligned?"**

Because let's be real—**giving is great, but giving smart is even better.**

The Role of Risk & Reward in Numerology

The Golden Rule: Risk Management Before Risk Taking

Before we dive into the thrills of **high-risk investments, lottery luck, and numerology-based speculation**, let's get one thing straight: **Risk management is everything.** No amount of numerological insight can replace **a well-thought-out strategy, financial education, and common sense.**

Taking risks without a plan is like playing poker blindfolded—you might win once, but long-term success requires **knowing when to hold 'em and when to fold 'em.** Numerology can serve as your **financial compass**, but you still need to **understand risk vs. reward, diversify your assets, and never gamble with money you can't afford to lose.**

Risk Management by Numerology – How Different Life Paths Handle Financial Safety

Understanding risk is one thing, but knowing **how to protect yourself when things go south** is just as crucial. Different Life Paths **approach risk differently**, and their risk management strategies should reflect that.

Best Risk Management Strategies by Life Path

- **Life Path 1 & 8:** Use clear financial exit strategies—know when to walk away.
- **Life Path 2 & 6:** Stick to diversified investments and avoid emotional decisions.
- **Life Path 3 & 5:** Set strict loss limits—these numbers tend to gamble impulsively.
- **Life Path 4 & 7:** Slow and steady—these numbers should focus on risk assessment.
- **Master Numbers:** Must be aware of **overconfidence**—even great intuition isn't a financial plan.

Example: Ethan (Life Path 3) was riding high on a crypto boom, but his numerology advisor reminded him **to cash out in a Personal Year 8** before things crashed. He did—**and avoided a massive loss.**

The Psychology of Risk – How Numerology Affects Your Emotional Reaction to Risk

Some people can take a **major financial hit and keep moving**, while others **panic over a $5 stock dip.** Numerology affects how you **emotionally handle risk and financial uncertainty.**

Emotional Risk Responses by Numerology

- **Life Path 1 & 8:** Confident risk-takers but must avoid arrogance.
- **Life Path 2 & 6:** Overly cautious—sometimes missing big opportunities.
- **Life Path 3 & 5:** Emotional investors—prone to highs and lows.
- **Life Path 4 & 7:** Logical but sometimes too hesitant to act.

Example: Rebecca (Life Path 2) avoided investing because she feared losing money. Once she **aligned her investment choices with her numerology timing,** she started building steady wealth without fear.

Best Numerology Days for High-Risk Moves

Even if you're in the right **Personal Year or Life Path for risk-taking**, the day you make your financial move also matters.

Best Days for Investing & Speculation

- **Days that reduce to 1, 3, 5, or 8** – These are **strong for bold financial decisions.**
- **Days that reduce to 4 or 7** – Better for **financial analysis and long-term planning.**
- **Master Number Days (11, 22, 33)** – Ideal for visionary investments, but avoid emotional trades.

Example: Jack placed a **big trade on an 8-day** and saw **immediate success.** Meanwhile, his friend placed one on a **7-day**, and the market crashed hours later. **Timing matters!**

The Numerology of Financial Loss Recovery – How to Bounce Back From Setbacks

Losses are **inevitable in investing**, but numerology can help guide the best **way to recover.**

Numerology-Based Strategies for Financial Comebacks

- **Personal Year 1 or 4:** Start rebuilding slowly with safe investments.
- **Personal Year 8:** Best for bouncing back with **high-reward strategies.**
- **Avoid risky moves in a Personal Year 7 or 9**—these are **reflection years, not rebuilding years.**

Example: Emma lost **a fortune in her Personal Year 5**, but instead of panic-investing, she **waited until her Personal Year 8** to start fresh—**and doubled her returns.**

Taking the Gamble: When Risky Moves Pay Off (And When They Don't)

So, you want to **strike it rich**, but you also don't want to end up **living in your mom's basement** because of one bad financial decision? Welcome to the **fine art of risk and reward**, where numerology can help **tilt the odds slightly in your favor—or at least keep you from making completely reckless moves.**

The truth is, **some numbers thrive in high-risk environments**, while others should probably **stay far, far away from speculative investments.** Whether you're thinking about **lottery tickets, high-stakes investing, crypto, options trading, or even betting on a horse named "Lucky Number 8"**, numerology offers clues about **your natural risk tolerance and when to play it safe.**

Your Life Path & Risk Tolerance – Are You a Daredevil or a Safe Player?

Not all numbers handle risk the same way. Some people thrive on **volatility and speculation**, while others are meant to build **slow, stable wealth.** Here's what numerology says about your risk personality:

Risk Appetite by Life Path Number

- **Life Path 1:** Bold but calculated. Takes smart risks but doesn't always know when to quit.
- **Life Path 2:** Prefers security and partnerships—low-risk, steady investments.
- **Life Path 3:** Excited by high-risk investments but sometimes lacks discipline.
- **Life Path 4:** The most risk-averse—stick to real estate, index funds, and slow growth.
- **Life Path 5:** Adrenaline junkie—crypto, options trading, and gambling may be their downfall or fortune.
- **Life Path 6:** Values stability—best in real estate, long-term investments, and safe assets.
- **Life Path 7:** Overthinks everything—prefers research-heavy investments.
- **Life Path 8:** The ultimate **high-stakes player**—knows how to take smart, calculated risks.
- **Life Path 9:** Gives away half their wealth before they can invest it—better off managing philanthropy.

- **Master Number 11:** Visionary but prone to impulsive financial decisions—needs balance.
- **Master Number 22:** Knows how to build **massive wealth** but must avoid overleveraging.
- **Master Number 33:** Wealth through service and humanitarian investments—should avoid reckless speculation.

Example: Jake (Life Path 5) lost **half his portfolio in a speculative trading frenzy** but made it all back in **a single high-risk crypto trade.** Meanwhile, Sarah (Life Path 4) invested in **safe, slow-growth real estate** and never lost a dime. **Risk tolerance matters.**

Using Numerology to Time Your Risky Moves

Timing is **everything** when it comes to **high-risk investments, gambling, or making major financial decisions.** If you want the best odds, consider numerology's guidance on when to go all in—or when to hold back.

Best Personal Years for Taking Risks

- **Personal Year 1:** New beginnings—good for carefully calculated risks.
- **Personal Year 3:** Luck is high, but don't overdo it—best for smaller risks.
- **Personal Year 5:** The ultimate year for speculation, but also for **losing money fast** if you're not careful.
- **Personal Year 8:** The best time for big financial moves—high risk, high reward.

Worst Personal Years for Speculative Investing

- **Personal Year 4:** Slow and steady—avoid major risks.
- **Personal Year 7:** A research year, not a gambling year.
- **Personal Year 9:** A completion year—**don't start big, risky ventures.**

Example: Lisa took **a huge financial risk in a Personal Year 8**, and it **paid off massively**. Meanwhile, Tom tried launching a **new venture in a Personal Year 7**—and lost everything because **the timing wasn't aligned.**

The Numerology of Lottery Numbers – Fact or Fiction?

Let's settle this: **Can numerology help you pick winning lottery numbers?**

The Truth About Numerology & Lotteries

- Numerology can **help you choose numbers that align with your personal energy**, but it won't guarantee a win (sorry!).
- Some numbers have better "wealth energy" (6, 8, 22) and could **increase your lucky streak**.
- **The best time to buy lottery tickets?** Personal Years 3, 5, and 8—**but don't spend your rent money on them.**

Example: Michael started playing numbers that aligned with **his Life Path and Personal Year**, and he actually started winning **small but consistent amounts.** No jackpot yet, but hey—**profit is profit.**

High-Risk Investing – What Numerology Says About Big Bets

For those who love **stocks, options, futures, crypto, or speculative real estate**, numerology provides insight on how to **balance risk and reward.**

Risky Investment Strategies & Numerology

- **Life Path 5 & 8:** Naturally drawn to high-risk, high-reward investments.
- **Personal Year 5 & 8:** The best time to take calculated investment risks.
- **Avoid risky moves in Personal Year 4 & 7**—these years are for stability and research.

Example: David, a Life Path 8, **waited until his Personal Year 8** before making a massive stock investment—and it paid off **tenfold.** Meanwhile, Alex made a **reckless trade in a Personal Year 9** and ended up losing everything. **Timing is key.**

Calculated Risk vs. Reckless Gambling

The universe **doesn't reward blind gambling—it rewards strategy and timing.** Numerology won't turn you into a **Wall Street genius or a Vegas high roller**, but it can help you **understand when to take financial risks and when to play it safe.**

So, before you throw your life savings into **meme stocks, crypto, or the lottery**, ask yourself: **Is my numerology aligned for this move?** Because sometimes, the smartest gamble... is knowing when to fold.

Part 3
Mastering Investments & Wealth Expansion

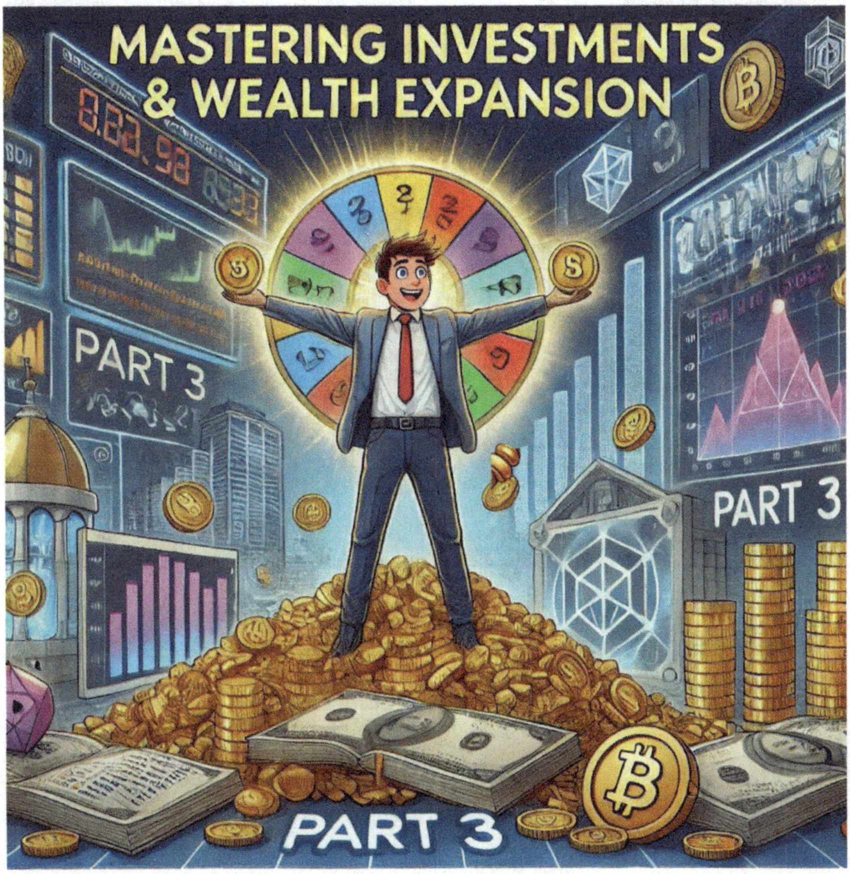

Trading with Numerology – Price Action, Breakouts & Fibonacci

Can Numbers Predict the Market? (Spoiler Alert: Kind of.)

If you think the stock market is just a chaotic mess of **charts, candlesticks, and financial jargon**, think again. Markets—just like everything else in the universe—follow patterns. And what is numerology if not the **science of patterns?**

Traders and investors have spent **centuries trying to decode the perfect formula for financial success**—from Elliott Waves to Fibonacci sequences. But numerology? That's the **missing piece** most traders overlook. Whether you're a day trader watching tickers like a hawk or a long-term investor **waiting for the perfect breakout**, numerology can help **fine-tune your strategy.**

But before you start **placing trades based solely on your lucky number**, let's dive into how numerology **aligns with market patterns, price action, and technical indicators like Fibonacci retracements.**

Numerology & Market Trends – Seeing the Patterns Others Miss

Markets move in cycles. **Bull runs, bear markets, corrections, breakouts, crashes**—these are all **predictable patterns** when you know what to look for. And guess what? **Numerology helps you recognize these cycles before they happen.**

How Numbers Influence Market Cycles

- **1-Years:** The market often sees **new beginnings**—startups thrive, fresh trends emerge.
- **3-Years:** Optimism, speculation, and **high volatility**—a great time for risk-taking.
- **5-Years:** Wild swings, big changes—stay sharp or **get whiplash.**
- **8-Years:** Financial powerhouses dominate—markets tend to **peak or correct.**

Example: In a **Universal Year 8**, the stock market **hit record highs**—and then, like clockwork, **a massive correction followed.** Traders who understood the numerology cycle **took profits before the crash.**

Trading with Price Action & Numerology – When Numbers Speak Money

Price action traders rely on **candlestick patterns, support/resistance levels, and market psychology** to make money. But here's what most **traders don't realize**—certain numbers tend to **repeat in price movements**, and these numbers align with numerology principles.

Key Numbers in Trading & Their Numerology Influence

- **1 (New Start):** A breakout forming, time to enter early.
- **3 (Momentum):** A strong trend gaining speed—watch for **breakout confirmation.**
- **5 (Reversal Point):** A pivot or correction is likely—time to hedge.
- **8 (Wealth & Expansion):** A **high-energy level** for big moves.
- **11 & 22 (Master Numbers):** Major turning points—pay attention!

Example: A trader noticed that every time a stock hit **$333**, it **either surged or reversed**. Coincidence? Nope—**3 is the number of expansion, and 333 amplifies that energy.** He started using numerology alongside technical analysis—and **his success rate doubled.**

Fibonacci Retracements & Numerology – Is the Market Really Doing Math?

If you've been around trading circles, you've heard of **Fibonacci retracements**—the magical sequence that traders use to **identify key support and resistance levels.** But here's the fun part: **Fibonacci numbers align with numerology principles.**

How Fibonacci Levels Connect with Numerology

- **23.6% (5-energy):** A short-term pullback—watch for reversals.
- **38.2% (Master 11 energy):** A significant retracement—major decision point.
- **50% (Balance & Harmony – 6-energy):** A psychological level, but **not an official Fibonacci number.**
- **61.8% (8-energy):** The golden ratio—where trends **often reverse or continue strongly.**

Example: A trader realized that **stocks reversing at the 61.8% retracement level** aligned with **Personal Year 8 cycles**—a year of **financial expansion.** Using numerology with Fibonacci, he **timed his entries and exits more precisely.**

Master Numbers in Trading – The Game Changers

Master Numbers (11, 22, 33) hold **special significance in numerology**—and guess what? They also appear **in market data, stock tickers, and even Fibonacci sequences.**

How Master Numbers Influence Markets

- **11:** High volatility—watch for major news-driven events.
- **22:** Market stability—strong consolidation or trend continuation.
- **33:** Unusual financial shifts—either a massive boom or a market correction.

Example: A trader started tracking **the number 11 in stock prices and indexes.** Every time it showed up on his charts, a **sudden market shift** followed. **Now he watches for it as a trading signal.**

Best Trading Strategies Based on Numerology

Numerology can **fine-tune trading strategies** so you can stop making **emotionally driven trades** and start **following numerical patterns.**

Best Trading Strategies by Numerology Year

- **Personal Year 1: Best for starting fresh portfolios** or trying new trading strategies.
- **Personal Year 5: Great for high-risk, high-reward trades**—but stay disciplined.
- **Personal Year 8: Ideal for maximizing profits**—focus on **long-term investments.**
- **Personal Year 9: A year to exit bad trades and cut losses.**

Example: David entered **a long-term trade in a Personal Year 8** and saw **massive gains.** Meanwhile, Alex tried high-risk trading in a Personal Year 4 (stability-focused) and lost money. **Timing is everything.**

Trading Smarter, Not Harder

Numerology isn't a magic wand, but it **helps traders see patterns that most ignore.** Pairing it with traditional technical analysis like **price action, Fibonacci levels, and market trends** can give you **an extra edge.**

So, the next time someone says, **"Trading is all about numbers,"** just nod and smile—because now you **really know what that means.**

Numerology for Different Investment Markets – Crypto, Stocks, Forex & More

From Wall Street to Web3: Can Numbers Predict Profits?

Let's be real: **investing can feel like gambling in a tuxedo.** One minute, you're riding high on a winning streak, and the next, you're questioning all your life choices. But what if numerology could help **cut through the noise and give you an edge** in different markets?

Stocks, crypto, Forex, futures—every investment vehicle **has its own energy**, and numerology can help you determine **which market aligns with your personal numbers and when to make your moves.**

Because let's face it, if your investment strategy consists of **random YOLO bets and praying to the market gods**, you might as well consult **something that actually follows universal patterns.**

Numerology & Investment Strategies – What's Your Investing Style?

Different numbers align with **different investing styles.** Some numbers thrive on the **chaos of crypto**, while others prefer the **slow and steady world of long-term stocks.** Knowing your **numerology-based investor profile** can help you **avoid unnecessary risks and maximize gains.**

Best Investment Strategies Based on Life Path Numbers

- **Life Path 1:** Bold and independent investors—best suited for **entrepreneurial investments, IPOs, and startup funding.**
- **Life Path 2:** Prefers partnerships—good for **joint real estate, long-term mutual funds, and stable dividend stocks.**
- **Life Path 3:** Creative and trend-driven—best for **volatile investments like NFTs and emerging markets.**
- **Life Path 4:** The ultimate long-term planner—**loves real estate, index funds, and blue-chip stocks.**
- **Life Path 5:** Risk-taker—**perfect for crypto, Forex, and speculative trading.**
- **Life Path 6:** Stability-focused—best suited for **ethical investing, community-based investments, and REITs.**
- **Life Path 7:** The deep thinker—**great at research-heavy investments like algorithmic trading or biotech stocks.**
- **Life Path 8:** Natural wealth magnet—thrives in **futures trading, commodities, and high-stakes investing.**
- **Life Path 9:** The impact investor—**drawn to socially responsible stocks and philanthropy-based funds.**
- **Master Number 11:** The intuitive investor—**best at spotting trends before the crowd in tech, AI, and alternative assets.**
- **Master Number 22:** The empire builder—**excels at large-scale investments, real estate development, and big-money moves.**
- **Master Number 33:** The ethical financier—best at **funding humanitarian projects, non-profits, and sustainability funds.**

Example: Ryan, a **Life Path 5**, tried the **slow-burn investment approach**, but he couldn't sit still. Once he shifted to **high-risk, high-reward crypto trading**, he started making **bigger gains (and losses, but hey, he loved the thrill).**

Crypto & Numerology – A Market Built on Speculation & Chaos

Cryptocurrency is basically **the Wild West of finance**—high volatility, **overnight millionaires,** and just as many horror stories. But here's the twist: **crypto actually follows patterns**, and numerology can help you figure out **when to buy, when to sell, and when to sit on your hands.**

Best Numerology Years for Crypto Investing

- **Personal Year 1 or 3:** Great for new ventures and speculative plays.
- **Personal Year 5:** High volatility—**big wins and big losses.**
- **Personal Year 8:** The **best year for major gains and holding long-term.**
- **Avoid Year 7 or 9:** Reflection and completion cycles—**not the time to gamble.**

Example: Sarah **invested heavily in a Personal Year 5** and rode a **crypto bull run** to incredible profits. Meanwhile, Tom jumped in **during his Personal Year 7**, just before a market crash. **Timing is everything.**

Stock Market & Numerology – The Long Game vs. Short-Term Gains

Stocks are a **more predictable** (but still tricky) investment. Numerology helps investors **time market cycles**, avoid **impulsive trades**, and **capitalize on bull markets.**

Best Stock Market Strategies by Numerology

- **Personal Year 4 or 6:** Best for **long-term, value investing.**
- **Personal Year 8:** Great for **aggressive growth investments.**
- **Personal Year 9:** Time to **cut losses, exit bad trades, and prepare for new cycles.**

Example: Jason bought **blue-chip stocks in his Personal Year 4**—slow, steady growth. Meanwhile, Kelly went all-in on **momentum stocks in a Personal Year 5** and had **the most chaotic trading year of her life.**

Forex Trading & Numerology – Playing the Currency Game

Forex (foreign exchange trading) is **all about timing**, and numerology can help traders identify the **best cycles for making money.**

Best Numerology Insights for Forex Trading

- **Personal Year 5 or 8:** Best for **high-frequency trading and big moves.**
- **Master Numbers (11, 22):** Great for **intuitive, pattern-based trading.**
- **Avoid Year 7:** Too much **uncertainty—markets behave irrationally.**

Example: Lucas, a **Life Path 8**, became a **successful Forex trader** because he knew how to balance **risk and timing**. He **only placed major trades in Personal Year 8**, and his portfolio soared.

Options & Futures – The High-Stakes Casino of Finance

Options and futures are **not for the faint of heart**—but numerology can help you determine **if and when you should play.**

Best Numerology Strategies for Derivatives Trading

- **Personal Year 3 or 5:** High-risk, high-reward environment—great for swing trading.
- **Personal Year 8:** Strategic, wealth-building year—perfect for leveraging options.
- **Avoid Year 9:** The **worst time for major financial risks.**

Example: Michael, a **Master Number 22**, traded **futures contracts in a Personal Year 8** and **made a fortune**. His friend, however, **ignored numerology timing and lost big in a Year 9 downturn.**

The Numerology of Market Crashes & Booms – Can We Predict Economic Cycles?

Market cycles follow **predictable numerical energy**, even if most traders don't realize it. Certain **Universal Years (1, 5, 9)** have been historically tied to **market crashes or major economic shifts.**

Numerology & Market Trends:

- **Universal Year 1:** Market resets, new trends emerge (e.g., 2008 financial crisis).
- **Universal Year 5:** High volatility—booms and busts.
- **Universal Year 8:** Market peaks, wealth-building opportunities.
- **Universal Year 9:** End of cycles—expect corrections and major financial restructuring.

Example: The **2008 financial crisis** occurred in a **Universal Year 1**, signaling a financial reset and the beginning of a new cycle. Investors who understood the numerology trend positioned themselves for the next bull run.

Using Angel Numbers & Repeating Patterns in Investing

Have you ever seen **repeating numbers on stock tickers, charts, or account balances?** Numerology suggests these aren't coincidences.

Angel Numbers in Finance:

- **111:** New financial opportunities.
- **222:** Time for balance—don't act impulsively.
- **888:** Financial abundance—often a sign to take profits or reinvest.

Example: A trader noticed his portfolio value always peaked at **$88,888** before a downturn. Now he sells a portion of holdings when he sees repeating 8s, protecting his profits.

Best Numerology-Based Exit Strategies – Knowing When to Cash Out

Most investors focus on **when to buy**, but **knowing when to sell** is equally important.

Best Exit Strategies by Numerology:

- **Personal Year 9:** The best time to exit bad investments.
- **Numbers 5 & 8 in stock prices:** Strong indicators for selling.

Example: Mark exited his **high-growth stock at $555 per share**—right before a downturn. He later reinvested during a Personal Year 1 and rode a new bull cycle.

The Numerology of Meme Stocks & Hype Investing – Should You Trust the Numbers?

We've all seen it—stocks that **explode overnight** because of social media hype. But numerology suggests some stocks naturally attract **high-energy speculation.**

Meme Stock Patterns in Numerology:

- **Number 5 stocks = High volatility, short-term gains.**
- **Number 8 stocks = Long-term wealth potential.**

Example: Dogecoin's rapid rise aligned with a **Universal Year 5**—high-risk, high-reward energy. Smart traders used numerology timing to enter and exit before the hype faded.

The Role of Birth Numbers in Trading & Investing Success

Your **Birth Number (sum of your birthdate)** influences your natural financial habits.

Best Investing Styles by Birth Number:

- **Birth Number 1 & 8:** Great at high-stakes investing.
- **Birth Number 4 & 7:** Best at long-term, data-driven investments.
- **Birth Number 5:** Naturally drawn to risk, must learn discipline.

Example: Warren Buffett, a **Life Path 8**, aligns his investing strategy with **wealth-driven numerology principles.** His long-term, power-based investments mirror his Life Path energy.

The Market Has a Rhythm—Are You Following It?

Whether you're **buying crypto, stocks, Forex, or futures**, numerology offers **a hidden roadmap** that can guide your decisions. The trick is **understanding the patterns, aligning with cycles, and never letting FOMO control your trades.**

Because in the end, **it's not just about playing the game—it's about playing it smart.**

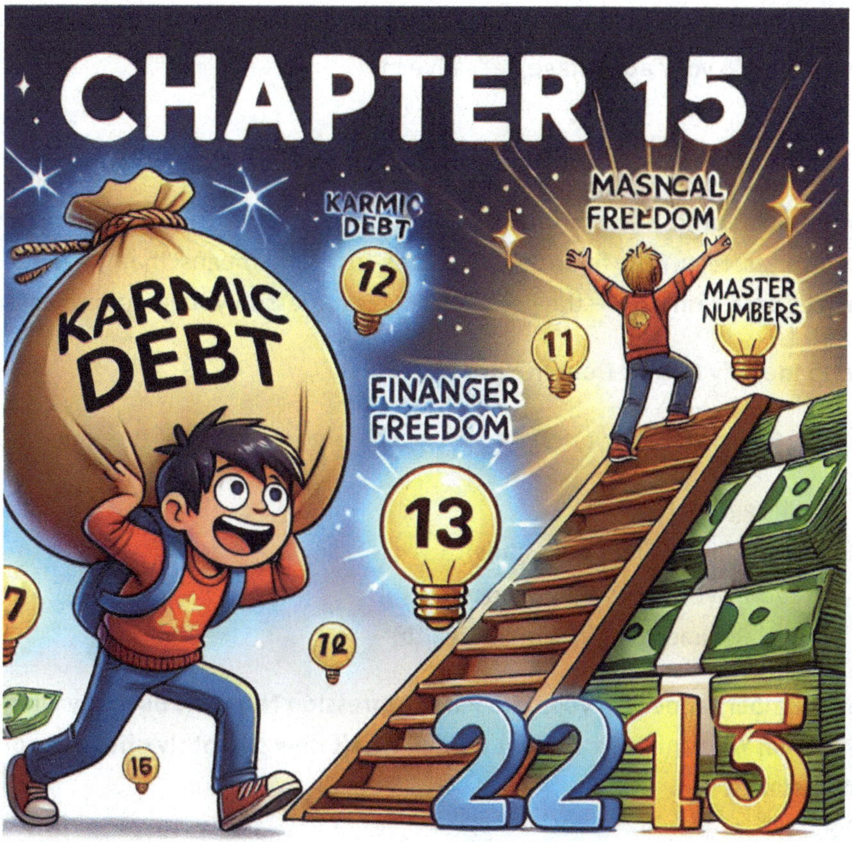

Karmic Debt & Master Numbers – Overcoming Financial Blocks

Is Your Wallet Haunted? Understanding Karmic Debt & Money Struggles

If you feel like **money keeps slipping through your fingers, investments mysteriously fail, and every financial decision comes with a side of regret**, congratulations! You might be carrying **Karmic Debt.** No, this isn't some woo-woo concept—it's a very real numerological influence that can **repeat financial struggles until you learn the lesson.**

On the flip side, if you've ever met someone who just **attracts money like a magnet,** they may be working with **Master Numbers**—the **big bosses of numerology** that bring both extreme challenges and massive financial rewards.

So, if you're ready to **break the cycle of financial struggle and start using numerology to your advantage**, let's dive in.

What Is Karmic Debt, and Why Is It Draining Your Bank Account?

Karmic Debt is **unfinished business from past lives or earlier life experiences** that manifests as **recurring financial obstacles**. It often means that **your money struggles aren't random**—they're part of a bigger **lesson you need to master.**

How to Identify Karmic Debt in Your Numbers

You have **Karmic Debt** if your numerology chart includes one of these numbers:

- **13** (Struggle & Hard Work)
- **14** (Instability & Financial Chaos)
- **16** (Ego-Driven Financial Collapse)
- **19** (Self-Reliance & Isolation in Wealth)

These numbers appear in your **Life Path, Expression Number, Birthday Number, or Personal Year** and indicate that **money won't flow smoothly until you correct past mistakes.**

Example: Mike had **Karmic Debt 14**, meaning **financial stability was a lifelong lesson.** Every time he saved up, an unexpected expense wiped him out—until he learned to **budget, avoid financial impulsivity, and embrace discipline.**

Breaking Free from Karmic Debt – What's the Fix?

If you have Karmic Debt, **don't panic**—it's not a life sentence of financial doom. The key is to **recognize your patterns and work through them with strategy.**

How to Overcome Each Karmic Debt Number

- **13 (Hard Work Debt):** Learn **discipline and structure**—stop looking for shortcuts.
- **14 (Instability Debt):** Master **financial planning and moderation.**
- **16 (Ego & Financial Falls):** Drop the ego, **get professional financial advice.**
- **19 (Self-Reliance Debt):** Learn to **balance independence with collaboration.**

Example: Sophia, who had **Karmic Debt 16**, kept making huge financial decisions **without consulting anyone**—which led to repeated crashes. Once she **hired a financial planner**, she started seeing **stable growth.**

Master Numbers – The Financial Superpowers (If You Know How to Use Them)

Master Numbers (11, 22, 33) are like **the VIP pass to the financial universe**—but they don't hand out wealth easily. If you have a Master Number, you're here to do **big things**, but success only comes when you **step into your power.**

Master Number 11 – The Intuitive Wealth Builder

- **Strengths:** Can sense market trends before they happen, intuitive investor.
- **Challenges:** Prone to **overanalyzing and hesitation.**
- **Best Financial Moves:** Trust instincts, but use logic **to back up decisions.**

Example: A trader with **Master Number 11** started noticing **recurring stock patterns before the market moved.** Once he started **trusting his intuition and using research**, his returns skyrocketed.

Master Number 22 – The Master Builder of Wealth

- **Strengths:** Can create massive financial success, strategic genius.
- **Challenges:** Can be **too controlling or overwhelmed by big ideas.**
- **Best Financial Moves:** Focus on **long-term wealth-building investments.**

Example: A Life Path 22 built **a real estate empire** by staying **consistent with his long-term plan,** rather than chasing fast money.

Master Number 33 – The Philanthropic Investor

- **Strengths:** Can **generate wealth for a greater cause.**
- **Challenges:** Tends to **give too much away, forgetting to sustain personal wealth.**

- **Best Financial Moves:** Invest in **impact-driven projects while ensuring financial stability.**

Example: A **Master 33 investor** made millions in sustainable business but had to **learn to keep a portion for themselves.**

How to Use Numerology to Unlock Financial Flow

Master Numbers and Karmic Debt don't control your financial destiny, but they **offer insight into how you should handle money.** Here's how to start applying these lessons today:

Numerology-Based Wealth Strategies

- **If you have Karmic Debt:** Focus on learning the lessons **instead of avoiding financial responsibilities.**
- **If you have a Master Number:** Step into your **higher financial potential**—but don't let it overwhelm you.
- **Align with Personal Year Cycles:** Avoid major money moves in **Personal Year 7 or 9**, but take action in **Personal Year 1, 5, or 8.**

Example: John, a **Master Number 22**, started timing his real estate investments based on **Personal Year 8**, resulting in **huge profits.** Meanwhile, Emily, who had **Karmic Debt 14**, learned to **budget before investing**, finally breaking her cycle of financial instability.

The Karmic Debt Money Cycle – Why Financial Lessons Keep Repeating

If you **keep making the same financial mistakes**, it's not bad luck—it's **numerological karma on repeat.**

How to Recognize a Karmic Debt Money Cycle:

- **Recurring financial losses** in similar patterns (e.g., always investing in the wrong thing).
- **Repeated financial struggles** despite changing strategies.
- **Feeling stuck** in the same earning/spending cycles.

Example: Sarah, with **Karmic 14**, kept **falling into get-rich-quick schemes** and losing everything. Once she realized **discipline was the key lesson**, she switched to a **structured investment plan**—and finally started seeing stable growth.

Karmic Debt and Business – Why Some Ventures Fail

Karmic Debt doesn't just affect individuals—it can **impact businesses, too.**

How Karmic Debt Affects Business Ventures:

- **Karmic 13:** Hard work, but burnout—businesses must **delegate and streamline.**
- **Karmic 14:** Instability—businesses should **avoid unnecessary risk.**
- **Karmic 16:** Ego-driven collapses—leaders must **listen to others and adapt.**
- **Karmic 19:** Self-reliance issues—entrepreneurs must **learn to accept help.**

Example: A startup with **Karmic 19 branding** struggled with **high employee turnover** and a revolving door of leadership. After adjusting the company's **name numerology**, the culture stabilized and profits grew.

The Numerology of Debt – What Your Personal Numbers Say About Borrowing & Loans

Debt isn't just about **numbers in a bank account**—numerology plays a role in how you **handle borrowing and repayments.**

Numerology-Based Debt Strategies:

- **Life Path 5 & 9:** Avoid unnecessary credit—impulsive spending is a weakness.
- **Life Path 4 & 8:** Use structured repayment plans—best suited for mortgages & strategic debt.
- **Personal Year 4 or 8:** Best time to **pay down debt aggressively.**
- **Avoid borrowing in Personal Year 7 or 9**—financial uncertainty may follow.

Example: A Life Path 5 who always **accidentally racked up credit card debt** finally learned to **budget better in Personal Year 4**, creating long-term stability.

How to Neutralize Karmic Debt – Financial Remedies Based on Numerology

Karmic Debt doesn't mean **you're doomed**—there are numerology-based ways to **clear the energy.**

Karmic Debt Clearing Strategies:

- **Changing financial habits** (e.g., structured saving for Karmic 14).
- **Aligning major financial moves with strong numerology dates.**
- **Shifting financial mindset** with numerology-based affirmations.

Example: Someone with **Karmic 13 struggles** who incorporated structured savings & daily financial affirmations saw **a dramatic shift in wealth stability.**

Master Number Pitfalls – When Wealth Becomes a Burden

Master Numbers bring **huge financial potential**, but also **major responsibility.**

Common Master Number Financial Pitfalls:

- **Master 11:** Overthinks every investment—must learn to trust intuition.
- **Master 22:** Takes on **too many financial commitments**—must focus.
- **Master 33:** Gives away too much—must balance philanthropy with sustainability.

Example: A Master 33 investor made **millions in impact investing but almost went broke giving too much away**—until they learned balance.

Numerology Isn't Magic—It's a Money Blueprint

Karmic Debt and Master Numbers don't **control your finances**, but they do provide **a roadmap for smarter money management.**

If you have Karmic Debt, **face your financial lessons head-on** and stop repeating the same mistakes. If you have a Master Number, **step up and use your financial gifts wisely.**

Because at the end of the day, the universe isn't punishing or rewarding you—it's just **giving you the same test until you pass.**

Business & Financial Success Stories – Learning from Wins & Losses

Winning, Losing, and Learning – The Numerology Way

If you've ever wondered why some people seem to **magically attract wealth**, while others are one bad financial decision away from starring in an episode of *Broke & Confused*, you're not alone. Success (and failure) isn't just about **luck, timing, or having a rich uncle**—it's about **patterns.**

And guess what? **Numerology is all about patterns.**

From self-made millionaires to financial disasters, let's break down real-world examples of **people who used numerology to make (or lose) fortunes.** Hopefully, by the end of this chapter, you'll be **taking notes on what to do—and what to avoid.**

Success Story #1: The Entrepreneur Who Built an Empire with Master Number 22

Meet Jason – A Master Number 22 & Wealth Builder

Jason was your **typical overworked corporate drone** until he realized his birthday reduced to **Master Number 22**—the **Master Builder** of numerology. He took this as a sign that he wasn't meant to be someone else's employee forever.

How Numerology Helped Him Win:

- Jason **launched his business in a Personal Year 1** (new beginnings, perfect for startups).
- He priced his services using **the power of 8** (the number of wealth).
- He strategically partnered with people who had **Life Path 4** (great for structured business growth).

Result: Within **three years**, Jason's real estate firm became **one of the fastest-growing in his city**, and he attributes much of his success to numerology **timing and strategy.**

Failure Story #1: The Crypto Trader Who Ignored His Personal Year Warning

Meet Alex – A Life Path 5 Who Loved Taking Risks

Alex loved **fast money and high-risk trades** (big surprise for a Life Path 5). He decided to **YOLO his savings into cryptocurrency** right before a major crash.

Where He Went Wrong:

- He made his biggest investment **in a Personal Year 9** (a year of endings—not beginnings).
- He ignored **repeating warning numbers (555)**—which screamed volatility.
- He didn't diversify—**all-in on one coin, no safety net.**

Result: Alex lost **almost everything** within months. **Had he waited for a better numerology cycle**, he could have entered the market at a **safer, more profitable time.**

Success Story #2: The Investor Who Timed the Market Using Numerology

Meet Olivia – A Life Path 8 Who Played It Smart

Olivia had **a natural instinct for wealth** (hello, Life Path 8 energy), but she didn't just rely on gut feelings—she **used numerology to time the stock market.**

How She Did It:

- She **only made major trades in Personal Year 8** (a year of financial growth).
- She **tracked Universal Years** and only went heavy on investments during years **that reduced to 6 or 8**.
- She exited a **high-risk stock during a Personal Year 9**, just before the market corrected.

Result: Olivia built a **seven-figure investment portfolio**, all while avoiding **major financial downturns.**

Failure Story #2: The Business Owner Who Ignored Numerology (And Paid for It)

Meet Steve – A Karmic Debt 14 in Business

Steve was **an ambitious entrepreneur**, but he had **Karmic Debt 14**—the number of instability and reckless financial decisions. His startup failed, but not before he ignored **every numerological red flag.**

What Went Wrong:

- He **launched his company in a Personal Year 7** (a time for reflection, not action).
- He **named his business with a numerology total of 5** (which is great for fun, but not for long-term stability).

- He **expanded too quickly** in a **Universal Year 9**, when businesses should be **wrapping up, not scaling.**

Result: Steve **burned through funding in under two years** and ended up in debt. Had he **used numerology for better timing**, he could have **avoided disaster.**

Lessons from Numerology Success & Failure

If there's one thing to take from these stories, it's that **numerology is an underrated financial tool**. Here's what we've learned:

Winning Strategies (Do These!)

- Launch businesses in Personal Year 1 or 8.
- Make major investments in Universal Years that favor financial growth (6 & 8).
- Use numerology to time exits (Personal Year 9 is great for selling bad investments).
- Pay attention to repeating numbers—especially 5s & 8s in finances.

Common Financial Mistakes (Avoid These!)

- Ignoring Personal Years when making big financial moves.
- Launching businesses in Personal Year 7 or 9.
- Taking high risks in numerologically unstable cycles.
- Ignoring Karmic Debt lessons—fix your money patterns before repeating mistakes.

Money Loves Patterns, and Numerology is a Cheat Code

The biggest takeaway? **Wealth isn't random.**

People who use numerology to **time their financial decisions** have **a serious edge** over those who don't. Whether you're launching a business, investing, or even just trying to break bad financial habits, numerology offers **a roadmap to success.**

So, the next time you're about to make a big money move, ask yourself: **Is the timing right? Is my number aligned?** Because, as we've seen, **when numerology and money align, magic happens.**

Future Numerology Trends – What's Next for Financial Success?

The Future of Money – Does Numerology Still Matter?

With AI managing hedge funds, digital currencies replacing cash, and blockchain creating a financial system that nobody (including the regulators) fully understands, the question is: **Does numerology still apply?**

Short answer? **Absolutely.** The financial world might be evolving, but the numbers behind it are still shaping our money habits, investment trends, and economic cycles. If anything, as we move toward **an era of automation and decentralization, understanding numerology will be even more crucial.**

Let's break down how numerology aligns with the **future of wealth, investing, and digital finance.**

Numerology & Economic Cycles – Predicting What's Ahead

Economies move in **predictable cycles**, and numerology plays a huge role in understanding them. Certain Universal Years are **historically linked** to economic booms and crashes. If you're still investing like it's a Universal Year 8 but the economy just shifted into a Year 9, **you might be in for a rude awakening.**

Upcoming Numerology Trends in Finance:

- **Universal Year 8 (Wealth & Power):** Economic expansion, rising markets, financial breakthroughs.
- **Universal Year 9 (Completion & Transition):** Market corrections, financial resets, major policy changes.
- **Universal Year 1 (New Beginnings):** Innovation in finance, new industries emerging.
- **Universal Year 5 (Chaos & Unpredictability):** High volatility—expect crypto booms, market crashes, and meme stocks dominating headlines.

Example: The 2008 financial crisis? **Happened in a Universal Year 1.** It was the start of a new financial cycle—just a painful one. Understanding these cycles can help you **prepare for the next economic shift before it happens.**

AI & Numerology – Can a Machine Predict the Markets?

AI is already being used to **predict stock movements, automate trading, and manage portfolios.** But here's the catch—**AI still follows numerical patterns.**

How Numerology Aligns with AI in Finance:

- AI-driven trading algorithms use Fibonacci sequences, a core numerology concept.
- Tech stocks often surge in Personal Year 1 and 8 cycles.
- AI-based financial decisions still align with numerology's predictive cycles.

Example: A hedge fund built **an AI trading model that accidentally followed numerology principles**—it bought stocks at Fibonacci retracement levels and used **algorithmic cycles that aligned with Universal Years.** Coincidence? Maybe. But profitable? Definitely.

Blockchain & Crypto – Numerology in the Decentralized World

If traditional banking is like an **old-school safe with a giant lock**, blockchain is like **a digital vault run by thousands of computers at once.** But does numerology apply to something as decentralized and futuristic as cryptocurrency? **Absolutely.**

How Numerology Influences Crypto Trends:

- **Bitcoin cycles align with numerology patterns**—it often peaks in Universal Years 5 and 8 (risk and wealth cycles).
- **Repeating numbers in crypto prices indicate key resistance/support levels.**
- **Launch dates of major cryptocurrencies often align with numerology-driven success numbers (6, 8, 11).**

Example: Ethereum's launch date reduced to an **8-energy** number—now it's the second most valuable cryptocurrency. Meanwhile, several failed crypto projects launched under **chaotic 5-energy numbers** and collapsed in months.

Digital Finance & Numerology – The Future of Banking

With **cash disappearing, robo-advisors managing portfolios, and fintech startups replacing traditional banks**, financial systems are evolving fast. But even in this high-tech world, **numerology still plays a role.**

Numerology's Role in Digital Finance:

- Banks shifting to digital operations often do so in Personal Year 1, 5, or 8.
- The best fintech startups launch in Universal Year 3 or 8 (growth and expansion cycles).
- Even account numbers and credit scores align with numerology-based patterns.

Example: A digital bank launched during a **Universal Year 5** and faced **chaos, lawsuits, and tech failures.** Meanwhile, another fintech firm launched during a **Universal Year 8** and grew into a billion-dollar company.

How to Future-Proof Your Wealth Using Numerology

The financial world is evolving, but numerology can still **help you stay ahead of the curve.**

Key Numerology Strategies for Future Wealth:

- **Follow Universal Year cycles**—invest and exit at the right times.
- **Use numerology in digital finance decisions**—whether it's picking investment dates or choosing business names.
- **Align with emerging financial trends**—crypto, AI, and fintech follow numerical cycles, just like traditional finance.

Example: An investor who **timed their Bitcoin purchases** based on **Universal Year 5 and 8 cycles** made **huge profits**, while others who jumped in at random lost money.

The Future is Digital, But Numbers Never Change

Finance is evolving, but numerology **remains a timeless tool.** Whether you're investing in stocks, crypto, AI-driven funds, or simply trying to understand where the economy is heading, **numerology can provide a strategic edge.**

The key is to **recognize the patterns before everyone else does.** Because in a world driven by data, technology, and digital finance, **numerology might just be the original algorithm for financial success.

The 30-Day Numerology Wealth Action Plan

It's Time to Sharpen Your Pencils – Yes, There's Homework

If you thought this book was just for light reading, think again. **We're about to get hands-on, and that means you have some work to do.** After all, wealth doesn't just appear because you read about it—it happens when you **take action**.

This is your **30-day numerology wealth action plan**—a step-by-step guide to applying **numerology principles to your finances, investments, and business moves**. Whether you're starting from zero or already rolling in cash, this plan will help you **fine-tune your financial strategy using your personal numbers.**

So, grab a notebook, a calculator, and maybe a stress ball (for when the numbers tell you what you don't want to hear). Let's go.

Week 1: Understanding Your Personal Wealth Code

The first week is all about **getting your numerology foundation in place**. You can't fix your finances if you don't know what's influencing them.

Day 1: Calculate Your Core Numbers

- Find your **Life Path Number, Expression Number, and Personal Year Number**.
- Look at what these numbers say about your natural financial strengths and weaknesses.
- **Homework:** Write down 3 key takeaways from your core numbers and how they've played out in your financial past.

Day 2: Identify Your Karmic Debt (If You Have Any)

- Check if you have **Karmic Debt numbers (13, 14, 16, 19)** influencing your money patterns.
- Recognize bad financial habits tied to these numbers.
- **Homework:** Outline 3 action steps to break any negative money cycles you've noticed.

Day 3-5: Decode Your Financial Timing

- Identify your current **Personal Year and Universal Year** and how they align with major money moves.
- Determine the best upcoming months for **investments, career changes, or launching a business.**
- **Homework:** Make a list of financial moves you should make **this year**—and what to avoid.

Day 6-7: Align Your Money Mindset with Numerology

- Find **affirmations based on your Life Path and Expression Number**.
- Reframe limiting beliefs—stop thinking "money is hard to earn" and start believing **"money flows to me effortlessly."**

- **Homework:** Write (and repeat) a personal wealth affirmation for the next 30 days.

Week 2: Applying Numerology to Daily Money Moves

Now that we've set the foundation, it's time to **apply numerology to real-life financial decisions**.

Day 8-10: Track Your Spending & Identify Patterns

- Look at past **big financial wins and losses**—do you see a numerical pattern?
- Identify **spending trends** based on Personal Years or repeating numbers.
- **Homework:** Create a financial journal tracking **where your money goes** for the next week.

Day 11-14: Choosing the Right Dates for Major Financial Moves

- Plan out when to **sign contracts, make investments, or buy/sell property**.
- Avoid making major decisions on dates that don't align with **your Personal or Universal Year**.
- **Homework:** Pick 3 major financial actions you want to take this year and determine their ideal numerology dates.

Week 3: Business & Investing with Numerology

For those with **businesses, side hustles, or investments**, this week is all about maximizing wealth potential.

Day 15-17: Name Numerology for Wealth

- If you own a business, calculate your **business name's numerology number**.
- If it doesn't align with **wealth numbers (6, 8, 22),** consider tweaks or rebranding.
- **Homework:** Assess if your business name is financially lucky—if not, brainstorm small changes to improve it.

Day 18-20: Using Numerology to Pick Investments

- Research whether stocks, real estate, or digital assets align with numerology trends.
- Use Personal Years and Universal Years to **time your investments.**
- **Homework:** Choose one investment and analyze whether it's numerologically favorable.

Day 21: Avoiding Financial Pitfalls with Numerology

- Recognize when **not** to make money moves (Personal Year 7, unstable numerology cycles).
- **Homework:** Identify 3 past money mistakes and see if they coincided with bad numerology timing.

Week 4: The Master Strategy – Creating a Long-Term Numerology Wealth Plan

Now it's time to **put everything together** and create a sustainable numerology-based financial strategy.

Day 22-24: Build Your Numerology Wealth Roadmap

- Set **short-term and long-term** financial goals using numerology cycles.
- Identify which numbers should influence **your biggest decisions**.
- **Homework:** Map out your 1-year, 3-year, and 5-year numerology wealth goals.

Day 25-27: Create Daily & Weekly Numerology Money Rituals

- Implement **small, consistent numerology-based habits** to maintain financial success.
- Examples: Check Personal Day numbers before making purchases, use affirmations before big decisions.
- **Homework:** Design a simple numerology routine for daily money management.

Day 28-30: Review, Adjust & Celebrate Your Progress

- Look at what worked, what didn't, and where you need adjustments.
- **Celebrate financial wins**—acknowledge how numerology has helped.
- **Homework:** Write down your biggest numerology financial insights from the past 30 days.

Numerology Works—If You Work It

Numerology isn't a **get-rich-quick scheme**, but it's a **seriously underrated tool for financial success.**

By following this **30-day plan**, you'll start to see **numerology patterns influencing your financial life**—and better yet, you'll know how to **work with them instead of against them.**

Because at the end of the day, wealth isn't just about luck. **It's about strategy, timing, and knowing when the numbers are in your favor.**

Part 4
Final Mastery & Long-Term Wealth Strategy

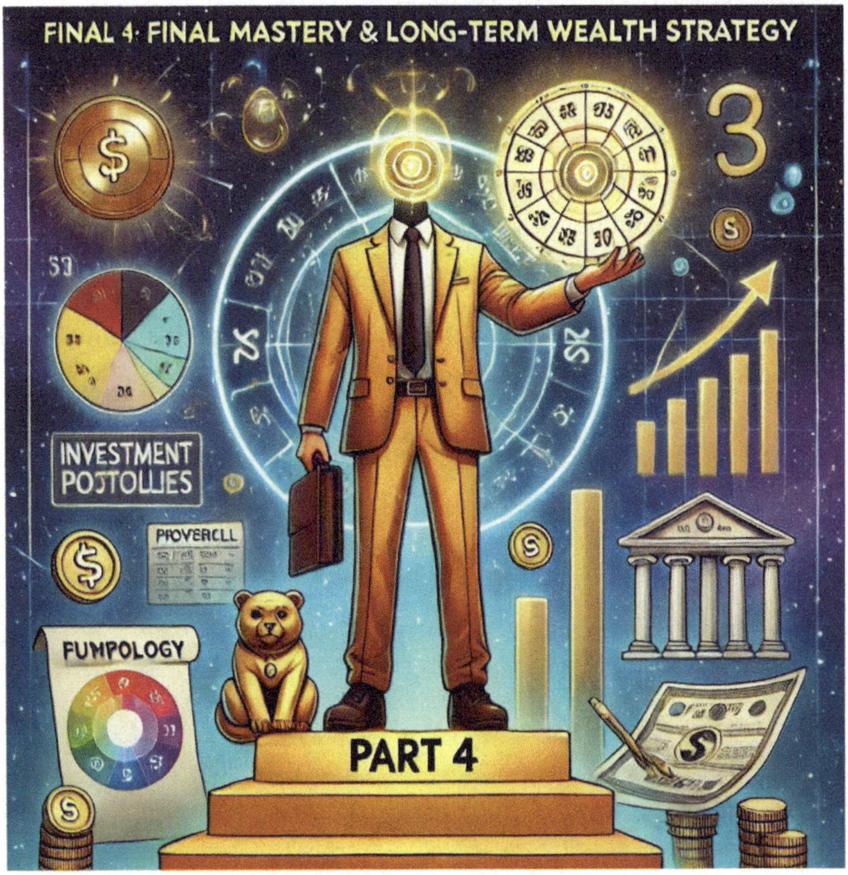

Creating a Wealth Strategy with Numerology

Hooray for More Homework!

Financial Planning Meets Cosmic Math – Yes, It Works

If you've ever wondered why some people just seem to **naturally attract wealth**, while others keep **accidentally overdrafting their checking accounts**, let's set the record straight: **It's not luck—it's alignment.**

Money follows patterns. **Numerology is about patterns.** So, it only makes sense that **if you align your financial decisions with numerology**, you get **a roadmap for success instead of wandering aimlessly through money mistakes.**

In this chapter, we're going to craft your **Numerology-Based Wealth Strategy**—a **custom plan** for aligning investments, savings, and spending habits **to your unique numbers.** Think of it as your **financial GPS, minus the annoying "recalculating" voice when you make a wrong turn.**

Step 1: Identify Your Financial Numerology Blueprint

Your Life Path & Your Natural Money Personality

Your **Life Path Number** influences how you **earn, spend, and invest** money. Before setting a strategy, you need to know how your number **naturally interacts with wealth.**

Life Path Money Tendencies:

- **Life Path 1:** Independent, takes bold financial risks, great entrepreneur.
- **Life Path 2:** Prefers **team-based investments**—thrives with business partnerships.
- **Life Path 3:** Creative but needs **money discipline**—can be impulsive.
- **Life Path 4:** The saver, structured, loves **slow but steady** investments.
- **Life Path 5:** Thrives in **high-risk, high-reward** investments—needs stability.
- **Life Path 6:** Invests in **home, family, and community projects**.
- **Life Path 7:** An analytical investor—**prefers research-heavy financial strategies**.
- **Life Path 8:** The **ultimate money magnet**—built for wealth.
- **Life Path 9:** A financial humanitarian—great at **big picture investments**.
- **Master Number 11:** Visionary investor—needs to balance intuition with logic.
- **Master Number 22:** The wealth builder—best at **long-term financial empires**.
- **Master Number 33:** Philanthropic investor—wealth strategy must balance **giving and sustaining.**

Example: Emma (Life Path 4) tried day trading and failed miserably. When she switched to **real estate investing and index funds**, her portfolio **started thriving**—because she aligned with her natural **money energy.**

Step 2: The Numerology of Saving & Spending

Saving and spending are **two sides of the same financial coin**. Numerology helps determine:

- **How much to save** based on your numbers.
- **When to spend** on big purchases.
- **How to make your money work** for you instead of disappearing into a black hole.

Best Savings & Spending Habits by Number

- **Life Path 1 & 8:** Save aggressively but **invest in power moves**—not penny-pinching.
- **Life Path 2 & 6:** Build savings **for security**—avoid emotional overspending.
- **Life Path 3 & 5:** Needs **structured savings** because of impulse-spending tendencies.
- **Life Path 4 & 7:** Best at budgeting—**focus on long-term security.**
- **Life Path 9 & Master Numbers:** Save, but also **plan for philanthropy & giving.**

Example: Mike (Life Path 5) realized **he was terrible at saving** because he always spent on experiences. Instead of fighting it, he **set up an auto-transfer into an investment account** so he could still enjoy life while growing wealth.

Step 3: Investing with Numerology – When & How to Grow Your Wealth

Best Personal Years for Investing

Numerology can tell you when to **go all-in on investments** and when to **sit back and wait**.

- **Personal Year 1:** Start new investments, launch a business.
- **Personal Year 4:** Invest in real estate, savings accounts—long-term security.
- **Personal Year 5:** Take **calculated risks**—crypto, stocks, venture capital.
- **Personal Year 8: The best year for major wealth moves.**

Worst Years for Risky Investing

- **Personal Year 7:** Research, don't act—financial clarity, not action.
- **Personal Year 9:** Wrap things up—**exit bad investments, don't start new ones.**

Example: Sarah (Personal Year 8) made a **huge real estate investment** that turned into a massive win. Meanwhile, Tom (Personal Year 9) tried to start a business and **failed because he ignored numerology timing.**

Step 4: Developing Your Long-Term Financial Numerology Roadmap

Now that you know how numerology affects saving, spending, and investing, it's time to build a **long-term wealth plan.**

Numerology-Based Wealth Plan

- Align major financial decisions with your Personal Year cycles.
- Match your Life Path energy with the right investment style.
- Use numerology to time career changes, purchases, and wealth-building moves.

Final Checklist for Long-Term Wealth

- Do you have a **numerology-aligned savings plan?**
- Are your investments **timed with your best Personal Years?**
- Have you structured your financial strategy to **match your natural money strengths?**

Example: Mark (Life Path 8) designed his entire **wealth plan** around numerology. He **only launched businesses in Personal Year 1, invested heavily in Personal Year 8, and avoided major financial moves in Personal Year 7.** His results? **Consistent financial wins.**

Wealth Isn't Random – It's About Alignment

Building wealth isn't about **guesswork**—it's about **knowing when to act and when to wait.** Numerology is a tool that **keeps you aligned with financial success,** ensuring you make **smarter, well-timed money moves.**

So, before your next big financial decision, ask yourself: **Is this move numerologically aligned?** If not, **maybe it's time to recalculate your financial strategy.**

Numerology & Financial Psychology – Mastering Emotional Intelligence in Money

Why Your Emotions Are Wrecking Your Finances (And How Numerology Can Save You)

If you've ever made a **terrible financial decision** based purely on emotion (*I'm looking at you, retail therapy after a bad day*), you're not alone. Money is emotional, and sometimes we treat it like an unpredictable, temperamental partner in a rom-com. **One minute, we're on top of the world, making smart investments—next minute, we're panic-selling stocks because the market dipped 2%.**

But here's where numerology comes in: **Your numbers hold clues to your financial behavior, emotional triggers, and decision-making tendencies.** So instead of letting fear, greed, or sheer impulse run the show, let's use numerology to bring some **logic, strategy, and self-awareness** into the mix.

Step 1: Identifying Your Financial Emotional Triggers

Your Life Path Number & Money Mindset

Your Life Path isn't just about what career suits you—it also determines how you **handle financial stress, risk, and reward.**

How Each Life Path Handles Money Emotionally:

- **Life Path 1:** Confidence can turn into stubbornness—might refuse advice even when needed.
- **Life Path 2:** Struggles with financial decisions, seeks too much validation from others.
- **Life Path 3:** Emotional spender—buys things for the "vibe" rather than practicality.
- **Life Path 4:** Hyper-cautious—may miss big opportunities due to fear of risk.
- **Life Path 5:** Impulse king/queen—if excitement is involved, money disappears fast.
- **Life Path 6:** Tends to put others' financial needs above their own.
- **Life Path 7:** Overanalyzes investments, sometimes to the point of **never taking action.**
- **Life Path 8:** Can get greedy—believes in money power moves but needs to balance ambition.
- **Life Path 9:** Overly generous—might donate half their salary before paying rent.
- **Master Number 11:** Intuitive but needs to balance **dreams with practical planning.**
- **Master Number 22:** Can get obsessed with control over finances—needs to **trust the process.**
- **Master Number 33:** Wealth means **helping others**—but personal stability comes first.

Example: Samantha (Life Path 3) realized she was an **emotional spender**, often buying **things she didn't need just to "feel good."** Once she recognized this, she set up **automated savings** so she could still enjoy life without wrecking her budget.

Step 2: The Numerology of Fear vs. Greed in Investing

Emotions drive financial markets. One day, **investors are euphoric, throwing money at stocks like confetti.** The next day, a market dip sends them **panic-selling like the apocalypse is here.**

How Personal Year Cycles Influence Financial Emotions:

- **Personal Year 1 & 8:** Confidence peaks—great time for bold investments.
- **Personal Year 4 & 7:** Financial fear kicks in—tendency to play it too safe.
- **Personal Year 5 & 9:** High risk-taking behavior—both good and bad.

Mastering the Emotional Rollercoaster of Investing

- **Don't make decisions on emotionally charged** days (check Personal Day Numbers).
- **Recognize when fear is driving you**—if you're selling just because everyone else is, **STOP**.
- **Use numerology timing to stay grounded**—trust your best investment years.

Example: Jake (Life Path 8) was prone to **overconfidence in investing**, making huge bets in Personal Year 5 (a risky year). He learned to **wait for Personal Year 8**, which was **better for big financial wins.**

Step 3: Avoiding Financial Self-Sabotage with Numerology

Common Money Self-Sabotage Patterns (By Number)

- **Life Path 1:** Won't ask for financial help, even when drowning in bad decisions.
- **Life Path 3 & 5:** Impulse spending ruins long-term goals.
- **Life Path 6:** Prioritizes helping others financially before securing their own future.
- **Life Path 9:** Too trusting—might fall for scams or bad investments.

How to Fix It:

- **Recognize self-sabotaging tendencies** before they cost you.
- **Align major financial moves** with numerology cycles.
- **Use affirmations to break financial fear** (ex: "Money flows to me in alignment with my highest good").

Example: Melissa (Life Path 6) had a habit of **lending money to friends who never paid her back.** Once she recognized this pattern, she set **firm financial boundaries** and watched her savings **finally grow.**

Step 4: Using Numerology to Build Financial Confidence

Confidence in money decisions doesn't happen overnight. But numerology provides a **structured, intuitive way to trust your choices.**

Numerology Tools for Better Financial Decisions:

- Use your Personal Year to plan major financial shifts.
- Choose numerologically strong dates for investments & contracts.
- Match your financial plan to your Life Path strengths.
- Set financial goals that align with your numerology cycles.

Example: David (Life Path 4) was terrified of risk. But once he learned to **invest in his strongest numerology cycles**, he built confidence in his financial strategy—and it paid off.

Money is Emotional, But Numerology Can Keep You Grounded

The biggest money mistakes **don't come from lack of knowledge—they come from emotional reactions.**

Numerology helps **identify financial triggers**, plan major decisions, and create a **strategy based on logic instead of fear.** So next time you feel the urge to make an impulsive money move, **check your numbers first.**

Because in finance, **the smartest investor isn't the one who knows the most—it's the one who masters their emotions.**

The Numerology-Based Investor's Toolkit

Welcome to Your Numerology Financial Toolbox

If you've ever felt like **investing is just a chaotic mix of random stock picks, gut feelings, and financial jargon that makes your head spin**, you're not alone. The good news? Numerology gives you a **system**—a **pattern-based approach** to investing that's been hiding in plain sight all along.

But let's be real. You can't **memorize every Universal Year cycle** or keep track of all your numerology-based financial moves **on the back of a napkin**. That's where **your investor's toolkit comes in**—a mix of apps, charts, and daily money habits designed to keep you **numerologically aligned and financially thriving**.

So, let's build your **numerology investing toolkit**—because if you're going to make money, you might as well do it with **strategy and cosmic precision.**

Step 1: The Must-Have Numerology Investing Apps & Tools

We live in a **digital age**, so you might as well take advantage of it. Here are some key tools to **track, plan, and execute your numerology-based investment strategies.**

1. Numerology Calculation Apps

Let's face it—doing numerology math in your head **is not the move**. These apps do the calculations for you:

- **Numerology Calculator+** – Calculates Life Path, Expression, and Personal Year numbers instantly.
- **Astro-Num Forecast** – Merges astrology and numerology for financial timing.
- **Lucky Numbers Daily** – Helps pick the best dates for investments, business launches, or contract signings.

---

2. Investment Tracking Apps (That Play Well with Numerology)

- **Wealth Tracker Pro** – Allows you to set financial goals based on **Personal Year cycles.**
- **Crypto Cycles** – Helps track **numerology-based crypto trends** (because, let's be real, crypto is its own kind of magic).
- **Stock Numerics** – A stock market analysis tool that factors in **Universal Year patterns.**

---

3. Digital Tools for Wealth Alignment

- **Wealth Mindset Affirmation Apps** – Daily reminders to keep your financial thoughts positive.
- **Personal Year Calendar Generator** – Plots your best financial months based on numerology.

- **Fibonacci & Numerology Chart Overlays** – For tracking investments alongside universal patterns.

Example: Lisa (Life Path 7) used **Stock Numerics** to track stock market patterns alongside **her Personal Year cycles**. She noticed that every **Personal Year 5**, she got too impatient and lost money—so she started **holding instead of panic-selling** during that cycle, and her profits **skyrocketed.**

Step 2: Daily Numerology-Based Wealth Practices

You don't need **hours of deep meditation or a shrine of lucky numbers** to integrate numerology into your daily financial life. Small, consistent habits can **keep you in alignment with wealth.**

Morning Money Rituals

- **Check your Personal Day Number** – Plan financial decisions accordingly.
- **Numerology-Based Gratitude Practice** – Thank the universe for financial abundance daily.
- **Quick Wealth Affirmations** – Example: *"Money flows to me in alignment with my highest good."*

Weekly Financial Alignment Tasks

- **Review your numerology cycles** – Are you in a financial expansion or contraction phase?
- **Plan your upcoming investments or savings moves** based on your numbers.
- **Declutter financial chaos** – Unsubscribe from unnecessary expenses, set automated savings.

Monthly Numerology Wealth Check-In

- **Analyze your spending & investment habits for patterns.**
- **Check the Universal Month Number** – Align major financial moves accordingly.
- **Reset your financial goals** based on your Personal Year progress.

Example: Jordan (Life Path 8) started a **morning numerology money check-in routine.** He **checked his Personal Day Number before making big financial decisions**, and within months, he felt more **in control and less anxious about money.**

Step 3: Using Charts & Cycles for Wealth Mastery

If you want to take your numerology investing to **a pro level**, you need to **start tracking financial patterns** like a boss. **Charts make this easy.**

Key Numerology Wealth Tracking Charts

- **Personal Year Financial Planner** – Maps out your best and worst financial months.
- **Universal Year Market Tracker** – Helps predict market shifts.
- **Fibonacci Retracements & Numerology Overlay** – For serious investors looking to time their trades.

Why This Matters

When you **track past money moves**, you start noticing **clear patterns**—so you can stop making the same mistakes **over and over.**

Example: Ethan (Life Path 4) started using a **Universal Year Market Tracker** and noticed that **his best stock market wins always happened in Universal Year 8.** He used this insight to **increase his investments during those years and reduce risk during Universal Year 5.**

Step 4: How Master Numbers Can Supercharge Your Wealth Practices

If you have **Master Numbers (11, 22, or 33) anywhere in your numerology chart**, your financial strategy **needs a special approach.**

Master Number Wealth Strategies:

- **Master Number 11:** Visionary investor—trusts intuition but needs structure.
- **Master Number 22:** The wealth builder—long-term financial empire focus.

- **Master Number 33:** Philanthropic wealth—money is a tool for impact, not just profit.

Example: Samantha (Master Number 22) struggled with **financial overwhelm**—she wanted to build wealth **but kept overcomplicating everything**. Once she focused on **long-term investments instead of short-term risks**, her **financial stress disappeared.**

Your Numerology Wealth Toolkit is Only as Good as How You Use It

Let's be honest—having a financial toolkit means nothing if you don't use it.

Your numerology-based investor's toolkit is designed to help you **track, plan, and execute your financial strategy with confidence.** But ultimately, **it's up to you to put the insights into action.**

So, before you make another impulsive money decision, ask yourself: **"Am I using my tools, or am I winging it?"** Because in investing—just like in life—**alignment beats randomness every time.**

Mastering Wealth Through Numerology – Final Success Plan

Mastering Wealth Through Numerology – Final Success Plan

So, You Want to Be Rich? Let's Make It Happen.

After 21 chapters of decoding numbers, dodging financial disasters, and strategizing your wealth moves **like a numerology pro**, we've finally arrived. This is where we tie it all together—where theory meets practice, and where your bank account **stops looking like a sad joke and starts looking like a power move.**

You now know how to align your money mindset, investments, and business moves **with the cycles of numerology**. But here's the catch—**knowledge means nothing without action.**

So, before we wrap this up, let's build your **Final Numerology Wealth Mastery Plan**—a step-by-step guide to ensuring your financial future is set, aligned, and growing in the right direction.

Step 1: Your Numerology-Based Financial Roadmap

Your Personal Wealth Blueprint by Life Path

Your **Life Path Number** determines how you should approach long-term wealth. If you've been ignoring your number's natural tendencies, **congratulations, that's why you're still broke.**

Best Long-Term Wealth Strategies for Each Life Path

- **Life Path 1:** Take **calculated risks**, launch your own business, and stop trying to do everything solo—strategic partnerships will take you further.
- **Life Path 2:** Build wealth through **joint ventures, real estate partnerships, and passive income streams.**
- **Life Path 3:** Focus on **creative industries, media, or influencer-based income**—but learn to budget, or your wealth will slip through your fingers.
- **Life Path 4:** Stick to **real estate, long-term investments, and steady growth strategies**—no need for unnecessary risks.
- **Life Path 5:** Balance **high-risk ventures with secure investments**—your energy thrives on excitement, but you still need a safety net.
- **Life Path 6: Invest in property, home-based businesses, or community-based projects**—your stability attracts financial success.
- **Life Path 7:** Use **data-driven investing, long-term research, and passive income strategies**—your patience pays off.
- **Life Path 8:** Build an **empire**—entrepreneurship, big investments, and power moves suit you, but don't let greed get in the way.
- **Life Path 9:** Focus on **investments that align with your purpose**—philanthropy and sustainable businesses will be your wealth sweet spot.

- **Master Number 11:** Your **intuition is your secret weapon**—balance spiritual alignment with financial practicality.
- **Master Number 22:** You're here to **build generational wealth**—play the long game, think global, and scale strategically.
- **Master Number 33:** Your wealth needs to be **impactful**—focus on money as a tool for positive influence and sustainable success.

Example: Matt (Life Path 4) realized that **his day trading obsession was draining him**—once he switched to real estate and dividend stocks, **his wealth finally started compounding.**

Step 2: Aligning with Universal & Personal Year Cycles for Long-Term Success

Best Universal Years for Expanding Wealth

- **Universal Year 1:** Perfect for launching a business, new investments.
- **Universal Year 5:** Risky but high-reward—if you play it smart.
- **Universal Year 8: Best year for financial success**—go all in.

Years to Be Cautious

- **Universal Year 7:** Focus on learning, not investing.
- **Universal Year 9:** Close old chapters, don't start new financial ventures.

Your Personal Year & Long-Term Wealth Moves

Align your **Personal Year** to time major financial decisions:

- **Personal Year 1: Set up long-term investments.**
- **Personal Year 4: Focus on financial stability.**
- **Personal Year 8: Expand aggressively, wealth flows easily.**

- **Personal Year 9: Exit bad investments, wrap up financial projects.**

Example: Sophia (Personal Year 1) **started a passive income side hustle** that grew into a six-figure business by her Personal Year 8.

Step 3: Wealth Habits & Daily Money Rituals

A strong numerology-based financial strategy isn't just about timing—it's about **consistency**. Here's how to stay in alignment **every single day.**

Daily Wealth Alignment Checklist

- **Check your Personal Day Number** before making big financial moves.
- **Set an intention for financial growth** every morning.
- **Use affirmations** that match your Life Path wealth energy.
- **Track your expenses** and align them with numerology cycles.

Weekly Money Rituals

- **Plan investments** according to Universal & Personal Year trends.
- **Adjust spending & savings habits** based on your numerology insights.
- **Declutter financial distractions**—get rid of things that aren't serving your wealth growth.

Example: Ben (Life Path 8) set up a **weekly financial review session** based on his Personal Year energy—his wealth increased **40% in a single year** by staying aligned.

Step 4: Future-Proofing Your Wealth with Numerology

You've built wealth—but how do you **make sure it lasts?**

Final Wealth Expansion Strategies

- **Invest in assets** that match your numerology strengths.
- **Plan wealth transfers** based on numerology cycles.
- **Use your Master Number** (if applicable) to guide high-level wealth-building moves.

- **Keep tracking Universal and Personal Years** to adjust financial strategies accordingly.

Example: Derek (Master Number 22) set up a **legacy wealth strategy** that will benefit his children and future generations **long after he's gone.**

Wealth Isn't Just Luck—It's Alignment

If you've learned anything in this book, it should be this: **money isn't random.**

Numerology gives you a **structured way** to plan financial success that's **aligned with your personal strengths, Universal energy, and long-term wealth-building strategy.**

So, the next time you're making a major financial decision, ask yourself:

- **Is this numerologically aligned?**
- **Am I acting in sync with my Personal and Universal Year?**
- **Is this decision a reflection of my true wealth energy?**

If you can answer **YES**, congratulations—you're not just making money. **You're mastering wealth through numerology.**

Made in the USA
Columbia, SC
08 March 2025

54532209R00089